A Paradoxical Community:
The Emergence of a Social World in an Urban Renewal Setting

**A VOLUME IN
CONTEMPORARY ETHNOGRAPHIC STUDIES**

Editor: Jaber F. Gubrium, *Department of Sociology, University of Florida*

CONTEMPORARY ETHNOGRAPHIC STUDIES

Editor: **Jaber F. Gubrium**
Department of Sociology
University of Florida

For Mercia, Gil, Lee and Dana—
an Unparadoxical Community

A Paradoxical Community:
The Emergence of a Social World in an Urban Renewal Setting

by   HAIM HAZAN

Faculty of Social Sciences
Department of Sociology and Anthropology
Tel Aviv University

 **JAI PRESS INC.**

Greenwich, Connecticut   *London, England*

Library of Congress Cataloging-in-Publication Data

Hazan, Haim.
   A paradoxical community : the emergence of a social world in an
urban renewal setting / by Haim Hazan.
      p.   cm. — (Contemporary ethnographic studies)
   Includes bibliographical references and index.
   ISBN 0-89232-963-7
    1.   Community.   2. Neighborhood—Israel—Netanyah—Case studies.
3.   Community development, Urban—Israel—Netanyah—Case studies.
4.   Urban renewal—Israel—Netanyah—Case studies.   I. Title.
II. Series.
   HM131.H369   1990
307.3'416—dc20   90-4921

CONTENTS

LIST OF TABLES

ix

Acknowledgments

The people from whom I learned to draw a fine line between the notion of community and its reality are the residents of Arod—a sponsored neighborhood within an Israeli urban renewal project. Informed by social awareness, their personal disillusionment endowed the study with many of its properties, of which paradox and contradiction are perhaps the most prominent. It was the residents' acute reflexivity that divested the ethnographic focus on "community" of its taken-for-granted qualities.

Contrary to the disenchanted candor of residents, the blatant rhetoric of a community harangued by members of project staff and communicated in all neighborhood media, exposed the concept as a form of practical ideology. Both groups reflected in its behavior a discrepancy between community as a symbolic construct and community as a social construction between perceived facts and desired goals, and ultimately, between word and action.

It was the attempt to reconcile these contradictions and to comprehend the undercurrent links between differences that induced and propelled the course of the argument presented in this book. For having been given that intellectual impetus and the empirical opportunity to explore it, I thank the people of Arod—residents and project operators alike. I am particularly grateful to Mr. Avi Ben-Simchon, the Social Director of the local project, whose unreserved permission for me to attend meetings and have a free hand in the collection of material, allowed me to move about in and out of boardrooms and to talk to people without a shadow of restriction or suspicion.

The fieldwork was commissioned and funded by the International Committee for the Evaluation of Project Renewal. Their support was both financial and moral, but above all, academically ethical. No dictate of "recommendation" or "focusing" was imposed, nor was any form of intervention at any stage of the research applied. Dr. S. Spiro, who headed the committee, read the preliminary report as well as an earlier version of the book and made some valuable comments.

The project, which constituted one part of a triple anthropological fieldwork on urban renewal neighborhoods, was administratively handled and academically monitored by the Jacob Blaustein Institute for Desert Research in Sede Boquer. I am grateful to Professors Emanuel Marx and Alex Weingrod, whose support and encouragement made the study possible. I would like to thank all those who were involved in the preparation of the manuscript, particularly Mr. D. Navon for his meticulous and conscientious proofreading and indexing.

If this book possesses some intellectual merit, it is undoubtedly owed to the invaluable contribution—both in inspiration and practical advice—by Professor Anselm Strauss. I was captivated by the social world perspective as an analytic tool that could do justice to an unorthodox conception of fieldwork, which places at its core ethnography of a concept rather than an account of boundaries and networks. Professor Strauss' deep understanding of the issues underlying the thesis and his encouragement to handle them in the manner adopted in this book, made the challenge of writing an intellectual adventure. The responsibility, however, for the content of the following is mine and mine alone.

Indeed, the burden of this responsibility was borne and shared by my wife, Mercia, who together with our children Gil, Lee and Dana, gave me a sense of reality and relationship while I was preoccupied with rhetorics, phantom concepts and elusive imagery. It was through them that in spite of the argument, the meaning of community was rendered unparadoxical.

Introduction

Whether you read this book for its substantive information or for its contributions to anthropological-sociological research and theory, you will, I predict, find it exceptionally valuable. Its substantive focus derives from an ethnographic study of certain aspects of an Israeli government program, "Project Renewal," designed to eradicate poverty and its many deleterious effects in a depressed urban area and to replace it with a whole new way of life. Professor Hazan was struck during his field work with the very considerable stress and strain engendered in both the project personnel and the resident populations. He took these tensions as his central interpretive problem, and traces for us in absorbing detail a set of the profound dilemmas that lay behind them. We learn of their sources, their consequences for project personnel as well as the area's residents, and their impact on the evolving social structures associated with Project Renewal.

Professor Hazan was equally struck by the great relevance for all the participants of the imagery of "community." A term constantly used by them, it carried a multitude of meanings, just as indeed it does to social scientists themselves when they use it in their studies. Yet, rather than throwing aside as useless for analytic purposes such an omnibus term, Hazan turns it upside down, so to speak, asking why and how the project participants used the term and with what significant consequences. This way of viewing community turns out to lead directly to the heart of the project's major dilemmas and the events associated with them.

In his interpretations, Hazan is, I believe, struggling with how to conceptualize and interpret the social structures "within" which contemporary men and women live out their lives. Involved in this issue is how people are both constrained to act by the facets of the world they live in and yet by acting change their world to some degree. In part, this is what he means by "the dialectical interplay between sentiment and structure" that "engenders the various manifestations of the phenomenon of community." To understand the institutions and organizations that evolved in conjunction with Project Renewal, Hazan draws on both the explicit and implicit theoretical resources of the concept—and perspective—of social worlds. This gives a means for illuminating the nature of the project's major dilemmas faced by the project participants because of the interplay of sentiment and structure. Indeed, one of his major points is that "built into the social world perspective are the social mechanisms that make sense of the transformation from sentiment into structure." In spelling out the descriptive detail carefully, he demonstrates the usefullness of this way of viewing urban life, but also adds very considerably to the elaboration of what is known and theorized about social worlds.

What Hazan's ethnographic materials allow him to do is to propose a curvilinear model of "community qua social world," in which the researcher can eschew many of the usual preconceptions about motives, functions and boundaries in favor of taking the original structural conditions into account, yet can trace the emergence of social world boundaries, functions and motives "as a consequence, rather than a cause of a given set of social actions." In short, as we read his significant analysis, we are looking at the evolution of a social world with its emergent and fluid and paradoxical properties, whose members draw on various meanings of "community." This helps to provide "a cultural context within which the code of erasing the near past ("renewal") and create an alternative reality to be pursued and transformed into modes of action." Yet this social world is infused with "sociocultural materials" rooted in the various other social worlds to which these very same project participants belong.

You can see that this book is much more than just another ethnographic study—though a solidly constructed one—for it helps to move both anthropological and sociological theory in the directions that I believe they should move in order to make those better instruments for understanding contemporary life. Lest this sound too solemn, I end by saying that you will find in Haim Hazan's pages not only the sturm and drang of that life, but also some of the more delightful and sometimes hilarious moments in the project's expression of the human comedy.

Anselm Strauss
University of California,
San Francisco

Chapter I

Community—Concept into Phenomenon

Fuzzy, diffuse and equivocal as it is, the concept of community has claimed a vital, almost second to none, standing in socioanthropological thought. Further confusion is accorded by the preponderant profusion of the use of the term in everyday language and in all walks of life. If, indeed, we live by metaphors (see Lakoff and Johnson 1980),[1] then images of community constitute one of the widest semantic zones in our cultural thesaurus. It would take more than a list of lexical definitions to embrace the voluminous pool of meanings and characteristics attributed to the concept, and restoring to scholarly discourses on the subject would prove equally unproductive. The multitude of approaches and their nuances found in the literature on "community" would disarm any student of the subject from his panoply of analytic tools, and would render the concept even more perplexing, debunking it of any vestige of common-sense intelligibility it possessed before.

Intellectually frustrating as it might seem, the task of disentangling the properties of the concept must not be eschewed, for "community," with all its nebulous connotations and diversified usages—and perhaps due to them—is undeniably a significant cornerstone in the construction of both sociological and social realities. However, rather than asking what "community" means, we shall transpose the query and wonder "what it does." In other words, our point of departure assumes the existence of the term within the realms of social interaction, cultural idioms

1

and modes of interpretation; hence the purpose of our discussion is to examine "community" not as a consequence of commonly analyzable structures and processes, but rather as a possible cause for their emergence. We shall maintain that the treatment of the concept in the course of everyday life in a given context germinates a host of phenomena that, in turn, evolve into a dynamic, viable social reality. Evidently, this overly general proposition calls for specific elucidation. This will require a systematic exposition of the main premises upon which our approach is based and of the vein in which the argument is to be developed.

Notwithstanding the reservation hitherto expressed regarding the implausibility of sorting out the intricacies of the concept, it would seem more than a mere perfunctory academic practice to place our angle within the context of other perspectives on the subject. It might even serve as a rationale as well as a critical backdrop for the ensuing analysis. Furthermore, it will also provide the underpinnings for choosing analytic theoretical devices and their grounding in the particular case study at the heart of this book. The following, therefore, is not intended to be a theoretical preamble to an ethnographic account, but a formulation of terms of reference within which the description is imbued, and within which the elucidation of empirically grounded analysis is rendered attainable and tenable.

Indeed, the set objective of this chapter is to propound a way of reasoning along which conventionally-held socioanthropological views and concepts of "community" could be examined through the prism of community as a social phenomenon. Thus, the immanent properties of the conceptual framework of "community" as an analytic device will be compared to the attributes of the socially constructed symbol of community as a communicable code. At the core of the discussion stands the assumption that research into "community" would benefit from an attempt to ascertain the relationship between the two manifestations of the concept, neither of which informs the other, and both are often interchangeably employed to signify the reality of "community." Far from being an intellectual exercise in practical hermeneutics, the analysis aims at breaking a vicious circle in which folk models or emic nomenclature is inadvertently transformed into "objective" etic concepts and vice versa. It is my contention that if the reported phenomenon of community is to be analyzed as a unit of social experience, the concept of community as used in sociology and anthropology ought to be reconsidered.

The discussion henceforth stands to pursue this line of argument. Various usages of the concept of community will be sketchily illustrated to be followed by a counterpresentation of community as a socially-conceived phenomenon. This will be charted in a working model that is the basis for the ensuing section of the ethnography as a fitting case study for the problem at hand. The subsequent chapters, which constitute the main bulk of the book, are designed to present the argument and its components as emergent properties of the ethnographic material. The last chapter, while reverting to the conceptual framework of the current discussion, will highlight a number of ways by which community is amenable to serve as a sociological concept. Underpinning the book is the idea that by releasing community from superimposed preconceptions, a clearer perspective of both the phenomenon and the concept will emerge, enabling the student of such social realities to develop an open-ended approach of the constituents, relationships and implications ingrained in them.

Another objective of the analysis is to establish a dialectical link between structural dimensions implied in the concept of community and existential aspects inherent in the phenomenon of community. This will be accomplished by disentangling the main structural dilemmas embedded in the concept of community and extrapolating them to the socially constructed experience of community. Curiously enough, this logical enterprise finds an empirical counterpart in the ethnographic material, thus furnishing the theoretical edifice with empirical substance.

As will be seen, the reason behind this unexpected compatibility is not in scholastic juggling of facts and ideas, but rests with the concept of community being a direct derivative of an emic term, thus containing and projecting many of its "folk-model" properties. Whether such discourse could be applied to other emic-bound dual concepts such as family, class, role, and so forth remains to be analyzed. However, what allows for straddling the two domains of knowledge and experience, the sociological and the social, is more than a mere common origin. Rather, it is the operation of a dialectic, an interplay between two seemingly contradicting dimensions that generates and shapes both. This is the intricate relation between sentiment and structure, which, being present in all community-connoted concepts and phenomena, infuses them with meaning and stamps them with the dynamics and uniqueness worthy of study and analysis. Hence, whether as Stacey (1969) suggests, community studies are a myth, the *concept* of community, being a viable social entity, lends itself to sociocultural inquiry in its own right.

I.   THE CONCEPT: IMAGES OF COMMUNITY

Voluminous and variegated as it is, the concept of community can take shape within four contexts, each of them representing a pronounced image of the essential nature attributed to the phenomenon. Because all these images have been contrived not by philosophical purists, but by students of social interaction, the intricacies and contradictions of human behavior are reflected in all approaches to community, making each and every one of them into a web of dilemmas and ambivalences. Riddled with inherent incongruities, images of community can hardly serve as a rigorous analytic device, but rather as insights into various premises and conceptions on which concepts of community are hinged. Indeed, most of the following discussion draws on implicit meanings of the concept as elicited from studies whose authors seldom volunteered more than a mere smattering of knowledge or awareness of the preconception underpinning their research. The emergent facets of community, therefore, are themes along which images of the phenomenon are generated. The four frames of reference within which these facets can be defined and articulated are: the notion of boundaries, cultural idioms, functional structure and temporal perspective.

It is almost taken for granted that, with the exception of highly metaphorical usages of the concept ("the community of academics," and so forth; see, for example, Foode [1957]), community is conceived of as a boundary-bound phenomenon. This is to say that a prior condition for considering a group of people in terms of community is a shared territory that serves as a base for interpersonal contacts and for the development of common interests.

Nothwithstanding the complexity of the coordinates for delineating community boundaries, the very idea of a fixed set of territorial markers within which individuals operate as community members poses a series of problems.

For many students of community, simple societies, as well as institutional settings, present themselves as ideal cases for community studies. Based on the assumption that such social units are well-defined within naturally conditioned or man-made territorial enclaves scholars such as Stein (1972, pp. 230-250), Keith (1982, pp. 4-5) and Goffman (1961)[2] presuppose the inevitability of visible physical segregation as a corollary of social identification. Thus, "tribes," "total institutions" and purposely designed residential settings are deemed to possess the necessary, albeit not sufficient, prerequisites for the emergence of "community." This assumption is gravely challenged when isolation and segregation are not present. Here more complex and subtle criteria for setting boundaries have to be applied, and territorial consideration alongside other factors ought to be employed to set the scene for a "community study."

Coupled with political yardsticks, ethnic identities or ideological-religious convictions, the ecology of community is rendered complex and sometimes inextricable. Aware as they are though, of the problematics of community boundaries, many scholars would rather modify definitions than dispense with the whole concept. Thus Park (1952) identifies three "communities" based on three sets of boundaries: "biotic," that is, functional interdependence; "moral," meaning group identification and loyalty; and "spatial," meaning distinctive location. A more forceful recognition of the multiple realities of modern man vis-à-vis community is put forward by Luckmann (1970), who states: "Most of modern man's existential universes are *single-purpose communities*. They are built around one specific role of the individual. The definition of the role—which all members of the community perform—is clearly understood and fully accepted."

Notwithstanding the apparent contradiction in terms between the idea of community as a holistic, totalistic multiplex system of relationships and the unidimensional image contemplated in that assertion, the preservation of the concept, regardless of its analytic inadequacy, is intriguing and telling. If what is considered the prerequisite for any reference to community, that is, predetermined boundaries, is a seemingly false assumption, the value and the essence of the concept must be sought in other preconceived characteristics.

The viability of the concept could emanate from the cultural-symbolic images that it conjures up. Visions of unbounded solidarity and unison of spirit and action inspired many to conceive of community as both a generator and a guardian of cherished identities and core symbols. Community is supposed to efface and surpass diverse interests, conflicting relationships and personal idiosyncrasies to provide its members with a sense of belonging to and identifying with, to use Durkheim's term, a social representation whose temporal dimensions reach the past, be it historical or mythical, and extend into the future, be it foreseeable or millenial.

Community as an idea is very similar in symbolic standing to the village (see, for example, Cohen [1981]) or the ethnic extractions[3] as cultural idioms rather than concrete realities. Being a culturally pervasive overarching symbol (Schneider 1979), "community" is employed to describe almost any localized group of individuals who share an identifiable culturally acknowledged common denominator. Examples of this are: Hippies (Partridge 1973), American Jews (Wirth 1928), American Indians (Dozier 1966), middle-class Americans (Seeley et al. 1956), the aged (Jacobs 1974; Hochschild 1973; Keith 1980; Eckert 1983), and many more. The quest for unifying symbols of community-suggestiveness is apparently directly related to existential uncertainties and relative powerlessness embedded in those social surroundings. Most of the aforementioned studies draw on such predicaments as the main attributes of these groups.

The concept, therefore, is applied to groups in distress (minorities, lower-class inhabitants of impoverished residential areas, the aged, the mentally and physically handicapped), and to groups whose identity is threatened or eroded (Nasbet 1953). Community is deemed to provide a psychological panacea to the maladies of alienation in modern society through the pursuit of localized sentiments (Hunter 1978), maintenance of traditional symbols (Erasmus 1981) or the promotion of 'we-feelings" (Keith 1982).

As obscure and elusive as they are, images of community as a shared form of emotive expression are often enmeshed in social networks and institutional patterns, which, in turn, endow them with a regulated code of practice entailing organizational components of roles, norms of behavior and rituals. However, when the communal symbol overrides any other mode of social identification, community ceases to function as a viable construct and alternative labels are considered. From focusing on communal symbols per se (Moore and Myerhoff 1975) to elaborate social configurations, such as communitas (V. Turner 1969) and communes (Abrams and McColloch 1976; Hostetler 1974; Kanter 1972), the plausibility of a community transforming itself from or into a sect-like society is explored. This seemingly semantic conversion suggests a significant aspect in our ensuing argument, because it indicates that once the structural-organizational dimension of community no longer operates, the whole concept becomes defunct and calls for replacement.[4]

The issue of localized community sentiments is invested with an inherent contradiction, for community is both a concept that signifies cultural uniqueness in the sense of "cultures" suggested by Cohen (1982), and a term whose roots and consequences are anchored in a general cultural system (Warren 1973). Not unlike its related concept of "subculture," community is two-faced, contingent on a peculiar identity while deriving its justification and legitimacy from a wider cultural context. Claiming uniqueness and being furnished and sustained by the overall social structure, the concept represents a duality that only practical, pragmatic reasoning can resolve. This, indeed, is the third image of community—the functional utilitarian value of the reality of community.

The experience of urban life, having posed a tangled conceptual incoherency for students of community, has generated another rationale followed by yet a further surge in community studies. With the irreconcilable dilemmas of social borders (Ross 1975) and the ambiguity of community symbolism, a new axis around which the sociological legitimacy and the social viability of the existence of community in a complex society can revolve is advocated.

Notwithstanding Redfield's (1955) conviction that research procedures, as well as conceptual frameworks drawing on communities in simple societies, are applicable to complex settings, the complexity of urbanism prompted and diverted interest in community to a goal-oriented direction. This is to say that communities in modern society are construed as social devices in the service of certain not necessarily explicit, social objectives (Gottschalk 1975; Hillery 1968).

Seen from this point of view, the question of boundaries and culture is less important than the function and operation of community institutions. Power structure, allocation of resources, division of labor and social networks form the focus of attention in an attempt to understand and, at times, to remedy and reform loci of tension, "maladjustment," organizational follies and social disintegration. The approach is predicated on the assumption that in the absence of other resources, well-planned collective effort is likely to produce results where individuals fail (see, for example, Tilly 1973). Although the overt emphasis is on action, the purposeful mobilization of people and resources toward a given end is inconsequential and inconceivable without a symbolic commonality or, at least, shared sentiments, which in turn become also mere instruments.

As social structures vary with goals, there is no substantive theme by which this perspective can be identified. From "intentional communities" devoted to the preservation of a cultural heritage (Erasmus 1981) to sponsored communities for urban rehabilitation (Suttles 1972),[5] the range and scope of the rise and fall of such socially designed entities is only limited by the variety of goals, objectives and aspirations that man can set to accomplish.

Relationships in such settings reflect the fundamental contradiction of community within a complex context. If action and interaction are unidimensionally geared in a predestined channel towards a given end, reference groups become segmentally rather than totally relevant (Turner 1955), hence defeating the very idea of community as based on a multiplex set of contacts bound up by all-embracing interests.

A further complication is induced by the incongruity in temporal frames embedded in such social enterprises. Although sponsored communities are designed to regulate and mold certain ideologically politically desirable social processes, the life cycle of the inhabitants, the turnover of population and the collective biographies of diverse sections of it are rarely synchronic. This invokes the fourth image of community—the temporal.

Societal processes of urbanization fused into individual life cycles and interwoven with the dynamics of everyday interactions in a bureaucratically controlled milieu call for a developmental perspective on community. Such evolutionary approaches can be found in Lynd and Lynd (1937), Stein (1972), Arensberg (1955), and Frankenberg (1965)—all analyzing communities within the context of cultural and social change. Notwithstanding the obvious merits of such a perspective, its conceptual framework betrays its presumed contribution to the understanding of community. For if community is a unifying factor and, in a way, a mutable experience, the diversity of structures alongside the ever-changing processes furnishing them make for elusive, asynchronic and precarious temporal dimension instead of the stable enduring persistence with which the concept is so often imbued.

The inherent contradiction in the temporal image of community, like the dilemmas instilled in the ecological, cultural and functional aspects of the concept, converge to one paramount duality, which seems to constitute an unreconcilable schism within the very notion of the term. This is the dichotomy between the structural-functional organizational elements of the construct and its character of common interests, unity, oneness, and shared sentiments. With the former being divisive and differentially separative, and the latter unifying and levelling, the concept as a whole is riddled with inconsistencies.

It should be noted that this divergent nature of the concept could be detected along its sociohistorical development, as stated by Williams (1983, p. 76):

> The complexity of community thus relates to the difficult interaction between the tendencies originally distinguished in the historical development: on the one hand a sense of direct common concern, on the other hand the materialization of various forms of common organization which may or may not adequately express this. Community can be a warmly persuasive word to describe an existing set of relationships, or the warmly persuasive word to describe an alternative set of relationships. What is most important, perhaps, is that unlike all other terms of social

organization (state, nation, society, etc.), it seems never to be used unfavourably.

Cognizant of the admonitions adumbrated in this passage—to eschew definition and to avoid value judgement when dealing with the concept—the student of community might find himself intellectually unequipped to handle a phenomenon whose conceptual coverage has been removed. This problem is thrown into relief following research into social settings where the conflict between structure and sentiment are relentlessly apparent, rendering the explanatory capacity of the concept doubtful. Such are total institutions, agricultural settlements operating within a highly bureaucratized environment[6] and sponsored urban rehabilitation projects.

If, indeed, the analytic values of community are forfeited by the problematics and inadequacies of the images hitherto discussed, the question of the advisability of employing this construct in a descriptive and interpretative capacity can be aptly raised. It would have been an uncomplicated and, perhaps, foregone conclusion to dismiss altogether the usage of community as a sociological tool, had it not been for the omnipresence of the term in everyday interaction and intensely so within the context of settings self-designated as "communities." In other words, the unquestionable existence of community as a socially propagated phenomenon prevents us from treating it as a sociological nonsequitur.

II. THE PHENOMENON:
COMMUNITY AS A SOCIAL WORLD

That community is a symbolic kaleidoscope through which social facts are construed and shaped, will be demonstrated later. How the dialectical interplay between sentiment and structure (paradoxical as it may be) engenders the various manifestations of the phenomenon of community, will also be described. However, a discussion of this nature cannot take shape without offering some thematic underpinnings capable of transmitting the observable phenomenon through a conceptual prism that projects a socioculturally framed picture of community.

To treat community as a phenomenon is to accord it an ontological status, which is both problematic and unnecessary for the purpose of the current discussion. It would require rigorous investigation of the state of consciousness of those involved in the constitution of the phenomenon and consequently would invoke discourses regarding the meaning of the experience embedded in that process. Similarly, viewing community as a cultural symbol would allude to a preconception concerning the inherent viability and potency associated with such socioanthropological entities. Neither of these approaches, however, should be dismissed as conducive paradigms for the understanding of the usage of the term in the given research setting. Nevertheless, the observations on which this study is constructed suggest a third perspective.

As will be explicated, the term "community" is widely and extensively used to communicate images, exchange ideas and negotiate terms of defining situations and interests. Furthermore, the terms, being a newly introduced linguistic coin, supersede well-established but nevertheless discredited locutions such as "ethnicity," "deprivation," "poverty," and "distressed neighborhoods." As such, it is a recently acquired cultural channel of communication that confers legitimacy and respectability on previously stigmatized actions, interactions and individuals. The embryonic nature of the term within that context, coupled with the social implication engendered by its emergence, renders the application of a traditional phenomenological perspective unyielding. Likewise, in the absence of cultural wont, symbolic analysis seems too crystallized and somewhat pretentious to address the fluidity and ability of the manner in which the term is used.

Much can be argued in favor of an ethnomethodological nomenclature such as "practical accomplishment" or "bracketing," but the exigency of accompanying such adopted terminology with the whole array of preassumptions concerning the "reflexitivity" of "members" and the negation of cumulative experience (see Rogers 1983, pp. 122-127) in creating situations, seems to overburden such an attempt with a load of theoretical predicaments.

Essential to any chosen conceptual framework through which usages of "community" are to be examined, is its potential to be grounded in the observable experience of the people under study, while at the same time offering an insight into the meaning of the ethnographic accounts. Here a fit between the required descriptive-analytic device and the sociocultural context of the setting in question is vital. In the particular case study upon which this book is based, the urban reality, the political circumstances, the cultural underpinnings and the dynamics of social processes have to be reflected in the expediency of the perspective to straddle the world of the researchers and the domain of analysis and explanation; that is, to make provisions for the understanding of "community" as an active element in social interaction, while taking into consideration the bifurcation between shared interests and sentiments, on the one hand, and the emergent social organization and power structure, on the other. This has to be accomplished, notwithstanding the hitherto discussed pitfalls considering community as an analyzable concept.

It would seem that such a set of stipulations might only lead to an intellectual impasse, or worse still, to fruitless polemics and endless diversifications concerning definitions, meanings and other properties of the concept (the concept of "ethnicity" can be adduced as a model case in point. See, for example, Yancy, Eriksen and Lulcani 1976). Indeed, if ethnomethodological liability is deemed tenuous, whereas functionalist rigidity is untenable with regard to complex settings, the perspective most suited to serve our objectives seem to be one that offers a formulation of social organization and interpersonal communication without the bind of predetermined structural constraints in the form of institutional rubrics, such as family, religion, occupation and other social corollaries of closed systems.

One such proposition is the concept of the "social world." Originally contrived in the works of some of the Chicago sociologists in the 1930s as a response to the dilemma of community studies within a highly segmented context, the concept is articulated and developed by Shibutani and Strauss. Shibutani (1955) considers social worlds as configurations of shared communication in industrial societies, where actors are engaged in a web of reference groups imbued with diversifying processes and meanings. Strauss, however, reconstructs the idea of social worlds within a distinct phenomenological tradition—that of G.H. Mead—and in a series of publications elucidates the theoretical foundations and the analytic properties of the perspective and advocates its research potentials (Strauss 1961, 1962, 1967, 1978, 1982). The approach is employed as a core idea in a number of studies concerning the world of art (Becker 1982), computers (Kling and Gerson 1978), alcoholism (Weiner 1981), liquor production (Denzin 1977, 1978), photography (Rosenblum 1978) and the lives of the aged (Unruh 1983). Diverse as they are, all these studies attest to the efficacy of the notion in its application to symbolic communication in modern society.

As a working definition, Unruh's formulation of the concept seems most suited for the purpose of this discussion. A social world is thus "a highly permeable amorphous and spatially transcendent form of social organization wherein actors are linked cognitively through shared perspectives arising out of common channels of communication" (Unruh 1983, p. 14). This typification of the perspective, while avoiding any explicit commitment to symbolic objects, interweaves social organization with common interests within one framework of communication. Furthermore, the characteristics of a social world, including the dialectics between organization and interest, that is, structure and sentiment, are emergent properties of shared channels of communication. This point cannot be overemphasized, for the whole edifice of our argument is hinged on its validity. The fact that actors, through circumstances, constraints and opportunities, happen to be involved in a system conveying messages can potentially turn that system into a social world, and most important, is capable of inducing an open-ended array of other sociocultural factors.

The nature of the messages conveyed can be as diverse as the variety of human interests prompting their circulation and dissemination. However, their phenomenological status deserves some consideration because it spells a significant characteristic of the approach of social worlds in general, and its application to our study, in particular. Evidently, the sociological conception constituting the idea of a social world draws heavily on the intellectual tradition of symbolic interactionism, hence conferring a symbolic status on the communicated items. Be it verbal, aural or visual; abstract or concrete; cultural or social; ideas or objects; social worlds are deemed to be invariably composed of symbolic representation.

Without attempting to enter the maze of endless discussions concerning the problematics of symbolic reference and action, it should be stressed that the identification between symbols and the constituents of a social world is neither self-explanatory, nor is it always constructive to the development of that notion. Notwithstanding the myriad of disagreements among students of symbolism, it would seem that the least common denominator that can be said to bridge even the most polemic of views is the assumption that symbols (or, for that matter, signals and signs) are associated with "meanings," "significations" or "signifiers." Indeed, it is this association that infuses verbal utterances, as well as visual images, with symbolic properties. This crucial link between signifier and signified presupposes a coexistence in time and space between the two (for further discussion, see Sperber 1975). This is to say that not only are symbol and meaning mutually and inextricably dependent, but that the former is a misnomer without the latter.[7] Furthermore, without some conception of a culturally anchored self-organizing and sustaining relationship between the two, symbols are no longer informed by meanings, and hence cease as a viable phenomenon, consequently, they lose their analytic value.[8]

These two attributes of symbolic action are not necessary coordinates of a social world perspective, hence enabling it to address some of the problems concerning the usages of "community" as a communicable sociocultural message. Indeed, the strength of the perspective rests with the relatively limited set of preconceptions embedded in it, which nevertheless do not emasculate its interpretive power. Thus, irrespective of preconceived motives, functions and structures, social worlds map out a communition-based design for the emergence of social interaction. Even without implicit postulates regarding their meaning of the communicated items and the ways by which such meanings are constituted, the notion of social worlds offers a model by which ways of recognizing, knowing and generating reality could be ascertained.

As we shall see, "community" was introduced into the lives of the people under study as a somewhat meaningless—albeit nonsensical—cultural idiom. Through it and with it they set to create and make sense of a reality that revolved around the emergent connotations of that very concept. Hence, if we are to accept Sperber's (1975) assertion regarding the evocation of a signified by a signifier, that "evocation may be considered as the search of information that allows the reestablishment of the conceptual condition that was initially unfulfilled" (p. 143) as a general pararmeter of symbolism, then "community" cannot be incorporated into that paradigm. There was neither information nor unfulfilled conceptual conditions to be reestablished. Conversely, the process of organizing and recognizing a reality with the template of "community" was a novel experience wherein "signification" or "meaning" was continuously constituted, rather than reconstructed or unearthed. In complex settings, particularly those imbued with uncertainty and ambiguity, where past experience may prove to be futile, if not detrimental, such a view on the ways people negotiate terms with their environment is compatible with both the dynamics and the nascency of such reality.

It is through the interactions and emergent situations engendered by the preoccupation with a given social world, that a form of social organization is created. Hence the link between the leveling effect of common interests and the divisive nature of social organization. It is precisely at this juncture that structure and sentiment may be conceptually reconcilable. It remains to be seen, however, whether this assumption is attested to by the ethnographic material at hand.

Moreover, built into the social world perspective are the social mechanisms that make sense of the transformation from sentiment to structure. The fact that the concept of community is not contingent on a specific cultural system, nor is it conditioned by personal whim or an interactional pattern peculiar to a given setting, makes its social world omnipresent and yet infinitely manipulable. It manifests itself in the capacity of any social world to be subdivided into overlapping, or contained within, other social worlds; hence its potentiality to claim legitimacy and to compete over recognition and acceptance with other social worlds (see Strauss 1982).

Pinned on a communicable common denominator, the social world acquires an ubiquitous atemporal quality representing to those involved in producing and sustaining it a sense of being an autonomous system. Although the social worlds of art or collection (stamps, antiques, and so on) seem to support most cogently this observation, this rule of seeming immutability freed from the burden of the threats and the hazards of the future can be applied to other, less culturally eternalized social worlds.

The social world of community in the Israeli urban setting under study lends itself to the implications of these propositions. It is argued that, for various political and socioeconomic reasons, "community" supersedes the previously fostered social worlds of "ethnicity," "cultural deprivation" and "economic underprivi- ledge." This transition requires a powerful leverage to eradicate the past and to forge new identities. Far from being accomplished in practice, the social world of community provides a cultural context within which the code of erasing the near past ("renewal") and of creating an alternative reality can be pursued and transformed into modes of action. The actual coexistence of a number of social worlds, particularly those that are supposed to be relics of the past, but instead continued to furnish the reality of the present, make for constant shifts and permutations between "community," "ethnicity," "deprivation," "powerlessness," and so forth. "Community," however, is the one and only social world into which people can canalize cultural paradoxes, social contradictions and personal stresses fostered in their other social worlds. Hence, in view of the novelty of the social world of "community," the activities and images surrounding its production are infused with sociocultural materials belonging to social worlds that in content and structure, contradicted the very idea of "community." This accounts, to a large extent, for the self- subversive, somewhat paradoxical nature of the phenomenon of community creation in our setting. It also stands at the core of the curvilinear argument henceforth presented.

III.   THE SOCIAL WORLD OF COMMUNITY: AN INVERTED MODEL

Eschewing preconceptions of motives, functions and boundaries, the construct of social world lends itself to provide a strategic starting point from which processual patterns of behavior can be traced through their vicissitudes and to their feedback effects on the structure and content of the social world. This curvilinear model posits the emergence of boundaries, functions and motivations as a consequence, rather than a cause of a given set of social actions. Obviously, this approach by no means implies that conceptions of boundaries, function and motivation do not precede the incipience of the social world under study; it merely suggests that both ethnographic credibility and the explanatory merit of the conceptual device can be enhanced and validated by faithfully adhering to the material at hand and by avoiding unsubstantiated preassumptions.

However, circumspect as one can be, some prefieldwork conditions must be considered to bring to light the backdrop of the emergence of the social world in question. Thus, although the ethnography sets out to explore the properties of the social world of community, the rudiments of the phenomenon ought to be sought in the social circumstances that bred it.

Three interwoven conditions cultivate the ground for the growth of community as a key social concept dominating the lives of the inhabitants of the neighborhood under study. The first was the novel introduction of the term as part of the newly fostered vocabulary of urban renewal in Israel. The second was the complexity of organizational structures and bureaucratic apparatuses involved in the "renewal" of the sponsored neighborhood, coupled with the fragmented and multifaceted experience of life in an urban setting in complex society. The third stems from the fact that conforming to the criteria of communication and exchange set by the bureaucratically sponsored objective of "creating a community" turned the concept into a valuable term in negotiating interests and in drawing available resources.

The first condition established a system of communication that was free of previously acquired stigmatic connotations and, indeed, drew on a set of much cherished values such as "modernity," "responsibility" and "participation." With discarded "dependency," "deprivation" and "ethnicity," community spelled acceptance and legitimacy for the operation of Project Renewal in the neighborhood. As we shall see, this code of approval and trust was put into ritualized practice by appointing residents as project officials and by devising recreational and educational schemes imbued with symbols of progress, revitalization and civic and national commitments. "Community" stood to represent all these, and as such furnished the second condition.

The second condition was one of conflicting interests, competing "small life worlds" (see Luckman 1970) and incongruous expectations. Its existence as a meaningful reality in the lives of the people under study became possible due to apparent coherence, tenuous though as it was, of the theme of "community" running through contradictory activities and rival ideologies. The notion of community was promoted as an ideal, overarching differences, embracing diversities and effacing conflicts. With Project Renewal being a nascent situation in the lives of the inhabitants of the neighborhood, as well as in the careers of its administrators, the need for an innocuous ethos for which fully-fledged support could be enlisted was pressing enough. But with the added complexity of uncertainty, such as the impending termination of the project (see below) and ambiguity, for example, ill-defined allocation of responsibility and over-fluidity of resources (see below), the adoption of community to satisfy this exigency became essential.

These inducements would have probably provided a most flimsy ephemreal basis for shared communication had it not been for the third condition. This is the introduction of community terminology as the only acceptable cultural idiom for the negotiation of interests within the framework of the operation of the project. It was instantly realized by staff members and residents alike that in order to put forward a claim, to participate in the distribution of public resources—services, financial benefits and career opportunities—the spirit of "community" had to be invoked. The reasons for this were embedded in the two aforementioned conditions, but the materialistic, interest-bound foundation that buttressed them endowed the concept of community with the strength and solidity necessary to propel its own dynamics and to ensure its perpetuation.

This is also the point of departure for the exposition of the modal argument along which the ethnography is organized and presented. After establishing that "community" is indeed an extensively employed, heavily charged concept among the incumbents of the setting in question (see next section), it is argued that the constitution of signification and meaning with which "community" is infused, draws on four distinct domains of existence. These are the boundaries of the ecology of the community; the cultural properties ingrained in the identity of belonging to the community; the control and limitation of resources and power associated with the community; and the transience and immutability generated by the temporal dimension of the community. It is hardly surprising that these existential domains correspond to the four images of community described in the first section of this chapter. Because the concept of community is an analytic device engendered and inspired by common "folk models" and emic perception, it could be expected that the social world of community would possess many of the characters of its sociological reflection.

It is further argued that the social world of community, like its sociological counterpart—the concept of community—is dominated and shaped by the dialectics of the two contradictory, yet complimentary elements of structure and sentiment. Each domain of the aforementioned four dimensions is an arena for that interplay, which, in turn, impregnates it with dilemmas and contradictions whose solutions are sought and exercised in various observable behavioral patterns. Indeed, the great bulk of the material can be construed as sociocultural reactions to the problems emanating from the self-contradictory nature of the social world of community. These problems, which by stretch of sociological imagination, can be considered foci of identity for the people under study, are elucidated in terms of four major dilemmas arising from and dealing with the four contexts of community.

Before proceeding with a description of these dilemmas, it is worth emphasizing that the issue at stake is not concerned with personal predicaments of individuals grappling with confounded images of reality. Rather, it is centered around structural inconsistencies and contradictions inherent in the production of community as a social world. Clearly, the behavioral patterns of the people studied reflect those incongruities and ought to be viewed as responses affected by their existence. Nevertheless, the argument gives causal precedence to the study of relations rather than relationships. It should also be borne in mind that the relations in question can be logically construed and treated as paradoxical in nature for, as we shall see, not only do some of them stand in direct opposition to each other, but one negates the possibility of the other. However, the intellectual turf required for any analysis in that vein is well beyond the scope of this study and thus, it is restricted in a more modest, yet not less cogent, terminology (for further elaboration, see Chapter VI, section II).

The first dilemma is instilled in the ecological context of "community." Here a well-delineated territorial enclave is designated to serve as the physical layout of the sponsored community. However, the incumbents of this geographically-zoned community are enmeshed in a great many other sets of sociocultural and ecological boundaries. Moreover, not only is the idea of territory as a community subverted by the residents' and staff's stronger involvements with other life-worlds, but the components of their selves deemed to belong to that "community" are selective. Thus social participation in local recreational activities is regarded as community-bound, whereas employment and kin relationships are excluded from that realm. Other aspects of daily life, such as education and political allegiances, are ambiguously defined and hence negotiable.

The second dilemma is a result of the neighborhood under study, being a part of the wider cultural context of Israeli society in recent years. The change of government that took place in Israel with the replacement of a labor-controlled cabinet by a right-wing coalition brings to bear the cultural position and the political power of eastern "ethnic" groups (see Herzog 1983). The advent of Project Renewal (see next section) puts these societal factors into organizational shape, and the implications for the dynamics of "community"-based symbolism are crucial. The idea of "community" is closely linked to the expressed desire to discard stigmatic elements of "ethnicity" and "deprivation". Thus, the panacea prescribed by the official social policies for accomplishing such a cultural purge is an ablution in "community" involvement. However, the materials for the content of such involvement are, in the absence of available alternatives, drawn directly from the pool of ethnic images, social problems and the nomenclature of powerlessness and dependency. Thus, by reinforcing "community" through the incorporation of other social worlds into it, the undesirable stigmatic elements are further highlighted, rather than dimmed.

The third dilemma stems from the resources available for engineering and building a "community." The attempt to establish a self-contained, relatively independent enclave of local government is based on a false assumption that outside intervention should be avoided and, in any case, can be resisted. The real state of affairs, however, suggests quite the opposite; namely, that the more autonomous position the neighborhood claims, the less it can rely on its own resources. Thus, having to draw on more external support in order to set up community symbols, such as recreational centers and care facilities, the advocacy of an autonomous community becomes a ritualized metaphor, rather than a viable social force. As the symbolic autonomy in the form of "community institutions" increases, the real intervention increases with it, and the gap between the idea of a self-sufficient community and the reality of a dependent neighborhood becomes wider.

The fourth dilemma draws on the temporal context of the setting. Images of community are propagated by various participants in pursuit of diverse interests in the course of implementing distinctly different policies. Notions of community espoused to corresponding fields of action generate temporal perspectives ranging from present-bound conceptions to exclusively future-oriented visions of community. This is complicated further by the imminence of the termination of Project Renewal, on the one hand, or the ominous prospect, for some people, of being trapped in it indefinitely, on the other. This throws into relief the core temporal issue embedded in the concept and phenomenon of community—that of implicit immutability constantly under pressure of external change and internal processes.

At the heart of our argument stands the postulate that these four domains of existence constitute four facets of the emergent meaning or signification of "community." Without such contexts and concepts, the idea of a community as a social world would lack substance. The effervescence of constituting meanings being fermented into situations molded by practical considerations is contained within given social constraints and available resources. As such, the social world of community engender systems of accountability, forms of rhetoric, images and needs that, in turn, could be analyzed in terms of boundaries, functions and motivations. This inverted model of community is rendered curvilinear by virtue of the vicious circle combined with the dynamics of macro and microsocial processes produced and sustained by the four dilemmas described. However, rather than being in a constant state of indeterminant self-perpetuation, the social world in question develops its own linear dynamics due to another inherent process, that of sentiment evolving into structure. The social interactions and situations furnished by the idea of community gather a forceful momentum, the thrust of which mobilizes resources and creates new interests. It is this dynamic-labile nature of the social world of community which this book set to explore.

IV.   THE CONTEXT—COMMUNITY AT THE CORE

The pervasiveness of community terminology in the setting under study can hardly be understood without considering the status of the neighborhood as a Project Renewal administered "deprived" area. A full account of Project Renewal and its place in Israeli society and among world Jewry warrants a lengthy study. The purpose of this discussion, however, can be appropriately served by highlighting some of the main features of the project as manifested in its official records, as well as in its public imagery. The former portrays organizational structures and financial considerations, whereas the latter attests to cultural codes and social conduct. Both, however, promote the idea of community as a cardinal theme around which the project revolves and toward its accomplishment it is geared.

Project Renewal sets out to replace the ruins of past neglect and deterioration with a whole new way of life. This aspired transformation is described by one of the students of the project as follows:

> No one variable can alone account for a three-decade long decay of neighborhoods in Israel. It is, rather, a whole system of interlocking and mutually reinforcing variables that has been inescapably leading to distress. Initial conditions of cultural

transition, poverty and poor education, the reluctance of elected officials to redistribute wealth, share power or invite popular participation, the poor yet arrogant services, the continuous withdrawal of the fittest from poor neighborhoods, apathy, low self-esteem, as other forces, are tightly woven into a predictable whole. One cannot simply add to this complex a new layer of local participation, responsibility, sensitivity and accountability; the complex as a whole needs to be replaced.

Indeed, the initial idea behind Project Renewal was one of complete reorientation. The ten-page outline of the *New Program in Israel 1978-1982*, later to be known as *Project Renewal*, analyzes the problems and suggests remedies. Despite the fact that networks of social services have greatly expanded, the report says, "Many groups of citizens and some locations and 'pockets' amidst us are still in need and distress." Government interventions to date "often reflect a rather chaotic patchwork of fragmented programs of housing, education, health, employment, personal and legal services, etc." The task is therefore to integrate the various efforts "...into a manageable and coherent human and social service system that is responsible to the needs of the people...there is now the need and the opportunity to restate our great and grave social concerns..." The restatement of the problem warranted, according to the New Social Program, a focus on neighborhoods. Although the main approach thus far has been to deal with social distress on the level of the individual families, the new plan advocates "an environmental treatment of human distress" not confined to symptoms of distress. Poverty, disability, lack of skill, absence of motivation, unsuccessful socialization and other "distress generators" are treated in this "comprehensive social program of community reconstruction."

The most important break point of this reorientation plan takes place at a rather early stage of the project. Resistance to change, coupled with power struggles among the Ministries, was resolved in a Cabinet decision that Project Renewal will operate "as an integral part of governmental ongoing social programs." In other words, Project Renewal funds are directed to the neighborhoods through existing programs. New policy instruments, which are warranted if the problem of distress is conceived in terms of neighborhoods rather than families, are thus "channelless." Rationalization appears at a later stage. The decision to implement the project through existing channels, and not through a special agency, a Project Renewal report says, addressed "...the need for continuity of the project after termination" (Deri 1982, p. 3-4).

Notwithstanding the ensuing political processes, the ideology of the project, being a totalistic comprehensive panacea for all past mistakes and misfortunes through the "reconstruction of community," prevails in official presentations and is built into the blueprint of the organizational mechanism devised to carry it out. Even the "International Committee on Project Renewal Evaluation"—an independent body set up to reflect objectively on the implementation of the project through a series of commissioned studies—presents the objectives and the organizational structure of the project in holistic terms of a major transformation (not to say conversion) into an entirely different mode of existence:

> The urban rehabilitation program known as Project Renewal was announced in 1977, as an attempt to improve the conditions of life in a large number of disadvantaged neighborhoods in Israeli cities. The program was designed to be an addition to, and not a substitute for, the many sectoral programs of the modern welfare state. From the start, the Project was a joint effort of the Diaspora communities, which were to provide expertise, as well as money, and of many separate government ministries. In most cases, Diaspora communities are "twinned" with Project neighborhoods.

In the spring of 1981, Project Renewal operated in 69 neighborhoods, selected according to criteria of social and physical distress and of the feasibility of effecting change. The total population residing in them is 480,000 persons, consisting of 117,000 households. Twenty-nine neighborhoods were selected in 1978, thirty-five more were added in 1979, and five in 1980. Resource limitations, as well as the need to consolidate the broad scope of intervention in both physical and social dimensions of rehabilitation, made it necessary to postpone the addition of the remaining 81 neighborhoods eligible for the Project.

Project Renewal is characterized by the multiplicity of its goals, the variety of guidelines and programs, and the complexity of its organizational structure. These can be summarized from official documents as follows:

Goals

- *Responsibility of the municipal authority* as a central factor in the rehabilitation process, as expressed in the planning, execution and follow-up of the various programs.
- *Cooperation with communities in the Diaspora,* at the government level, in the local steering committee, by means of the Jewish Agency and representatives of the communities abroad.
- *Employment of existing resources,* primarily by raising the level and scope of activities in existing facilities.
- *A comprehensive approach,* designed to activate and coordinate social and physical programs in the neighborhood, and to consider those factors and trends outside of the community that influence the process of rehabilitation and the future condition of the neighborhood.

Actions and programs

- Community organization.
- Development of family ability to provide household activities and mutual help and services.
- Enrichment of informal and formal education.
- Improvement of the extent and quality of public, social and commercial services.
- Elimination of crowded and substandard housing.
- Building of new housing in the neighborhood.
- Improvement of the physical environment.

Organizational structure

- At the government level: *a joint policy board* of cabinet members and the executive of the Jewish Agency for the formulation of general policy, and an *interministerial/Jewish Agency committee* to approve plans and allocate resources.
- At the local level: *a local steering committee,* chaired by the mayor, consisting of neighborhood residents (up to 50%), city

officials, Government and Jewish Agency representatives. This committee is in charge of the formulation of neighborhood plans and programs, priorities, and supervision. The actual implementation is supervised by the *neighborhood project director* in conjunction with the *manager of building and housing* (International Committee on Project Renewal Evaluation 1981, pp. 2-3).

Inspired by politicians, amplified by the media and furnished by interested parties, such as welfare workers and local activists, the rhetoric of community instilled in the project turns into a myth embracing the state of Israel, Zionist aspirations and the Diaspora. Like many other myths, it offers a narrative of creation and genesis interwoven into a timeless version of diffused social tensions and bridged over cultural diversities. Yet, pervasive and intensive as it is the advent of the project was meted out with a great deal of apprehension, cynicism and mistrust. Such criticisms are invariably leveled against the organizational implementation of the project with its complex bureaucratic infrastructure, rather than against the very idea of community orientation on which it is predicated. The following provides an illustration of the ambivalent attitude of anticipated redemption tinted with skeptical pragmatism catalyzed by the project.

As a piece of impressionistic journalism, the report must not be credited with infallible objectivity or data accuracy. It does, however, convey many of the reservations, scruples and social problems engendered by the project alongside eschatological praise and euphoric exhilaration.

A month after he was elected Prime Minister, Menachem Begin was to address a group of US fundraisers, all of them major contributors to Israel. A day or two before the scheduled talk, one of the Prime Minister's aides contacted the Jewish Agency to task which issues concerned these Americans, and what should be the theme of Mr. Begin's address.

The query reached the Agency's Secretary-General, Harry Rosen, a Boston-born social administrator who has spent most of his life in social planning and community organization. Rosen began to jot down some proposals for a project which he had been turning over in his mind for some time—a comprehensive social rehabilitation program, unique in scope and concept, whose aim is to eradicate poverty in Israel.

When Begin addressed the Americans he read from Harry Rosen's notes. 'Let me give you the figures,' he said, '45,000 families, nearly 300,000 people, live in abject conditions...It is intolerable to have in the midst of the Jewish people, in the heart of the Jewish State...such a phenomenon of poverty. We want to solve this problem once and for all.' Then he worked up to a ringing conclusion, 'We can do it, through a common effort by the State of Israel and the Jewish people all over the world!'

This was news to just about everyone: to the government; to all the ministries who were to be involved (education, welfare, health and housing); to the municipalities; to Diaspora fundraisers, from whom an additional $600,000 was sought. It was news even to Harry Rosen.

However, the announcement was made and the program entitled "Project Renewal" was launched. The manner of its birth explains a lot about the Project. It was born unformed and poorly conceptualized, and this resulted in incorrect emphasis and outright errors in its initial planning and implementation.

But the infant, struggling to survive clung on to life. The 'funerals' held last year in some Renewal neighborhoods, in which the Project was declared dead and buried in effigy, have proven premature. In the past 20 months Project Renewal has rallied, and it is gaining in credibility—if not in the Israeli media, then at least in a growing number of disadvantaged neighborhoods.

Project Renewal is the largest human outreach program ever undertaken by the Jewish People, and is one of the most singular outreach programs ever undertaken by any people. The Project's international urban renewal counterparts have often been limited to sporadic drives at selective aspects of community improvement. In contrast, Israel's version of urban renewal encompasses every domain of the lives of the residents in the targeted communities. The renewal has meant new roads, apartments, community centers, tennis courts, swimming pools, health clinics, youth centers, bomb shelters and street lighting. Where empty lots had stood, today there are well-tended gardens. There are cases where garbage dumps were transformed into playgrounds.

More important than these physical improvements are the new services which have been introduced. Where social programs had been nonexistent, there are now services for people ranging from pre-schoolers to the elderly. In fact, during the last two years, social programs have taken priority over physical renewal. Creative approaches to overcome community problems are flourishing, for example, programs exist: to aid young families in their parenting, to re-direct the energies of juvenile delinquents before it is too late, to offer special educational opportunities to children and adults, to provide activities for the elderly, to develop the first flicker of creativity amongst pre-schoolers, and to provide the medical attention some people have never had. In some communities adolescents, previously without any social outlets, can be seen taking drama classes, studying ballet, or attending a new scientific institute...

The program has already aroused the attention of many individuals and groups outside of Israel. Direct duplication, elsewhere, is probably unlikely. Resident involvement in specific community projects is not unheard-of outside Israel. However, the comparatively small size of the renewal neighborhoods in Israel made it possible to maintain the goal of total resident participation. This is a significant achievement by any urban renewal standards. The input from abroad would also be difficult to imitate. Project Renewal operates from an Israeli definition of poverty which is not typical of that elsewhere. Sofie Sasson, counselor for community workers in Jerusalem, says, 'Israel does not have poverty as such. No one, for example, goes hungry or unhoused. The problem is one of neglect, lack of self-confidence and poor self-image; all of which has resulted in over-whelming apathy.' However, in some respects, Project Renewal may well provide models for distressed communities abroad. Some of the innovative program concepts that have been developed in Israel may be applicable to the requirements of other cultures (Walsh 1982, pp. 21-22).

The vision of the project as a cultural paradigm befits the notion of community renewal as an existential resurrection implied by the magnitude, totality and intensity of the enterprise. The implications of such image on the Israeli internal political arena and on the relationships with the Western Jewish diaspora cannot be overestimated. However, the extent of the impact of this induced revival on its designated targets—the inhabitants of the "renewed" neighborhoods—is by no means a reflection of that spirit. Indeed, a comparative study of 20 project-administered neighborhoods concludes that although residents generally express a sense of satisfaction with the project, it is the material aspect of it, rather than the social, that wins their approval and appreciation (The International Committee for the Evaluation of Project Renewal 1984, pp. 21-23).

The neighborhood under study is no exception to this inconsistency between the objectives of the grand scheme and the everyday aspirations of the residents controlled by its social machinery. However, although striving to attain tangible gains, residents are mindful of the main cultural channel through which benefits can be obtained. Hence, the omnipresence of the vocabulary of "community" among residents and project staff alike. Such terminology is intensively used in both word and action to describe, explain and justify the life in the neighborhood. "Community," "community creation," "community institutions" and "community life" serve as a paramount linguistic code to communicate ideas and arguments, to protect interests and to convey messages. In fact, the vocabulary centers around the term community, and its ramifications and related concepts are adopted as a broad cultural common denominator in interaction among the people under study.

The language of "community" is so ubiquitous that it is used to transmit images of the neighborhood almost by everybody and in all walks of life. Evidently, such extensive reference to "community" suggests that there are multiple levels of employing the concept, with different initial meanings attached to each of them. Indeed, the "community" of the social worker seems quite different from the conception of the same terms as conceived by a local activist or a Project Renewal manager. A more thorough study of the various interpretations attributed to "community" unravels an ever more complex set of characteristics with intersecting meanings and changing interpretations, corresponding to vicissitudes of circumstances and contexts of action. In this respect Project Renewal has certainly left its mark on the neighborhood, for it seems that at least the sociolinguistic terms of reference and conceptual framework are fostered to shape and stamp the acts and interactions emerging under its auspices.

It is suggested that by reproducing a "community" and by inducing residents' involvement, the project, though its policies and institutions, generates insularity and increases dependency and further anxiety among residents. The underlying assumption is that the residents are fully aware of the pitfalls and risks ingrained in the project and adopt a whole host of stratagems centered around community manipulations to enable them to continue to benefit from the project without jeopardizing resources, positions and images at their disposal. This means that the various aspects of the project introduced into the neighborhood are differentially incorporated into it. This is to say that through a process of negotiation, arbitration and manipulation of ideas and images, the components of the project are sieved to be partly ignored, partly eliminated, partly accepted and, in any case, reinterpreted and accommodated to local needs and sets of relationships. It can be argued then that the initial stage in the development of community as a social world is manufactured by the "production of cynical knowledge" (Gouldner, Ritti and Ference 1977), which fuels the complex social process henceforth described.

In Arod, the pseudonym for the Project Renewal-controlled neighborhood under study, the marriage between the ethos of community infused into the imagery of the project and the practices of utilizing it as a local currency of bargaining resources, transforms an untenable myth into a gripping social reality. It is precisely this transition, rather than resources or values, that concern the following description of Arod's community-bound social world.

NOTES

1. The implications of their arguments to the study of culture are far-reaching. In the case of "community," it may contribute an important dimension to the understanding of the potency of the term as a powerful cultural idiom.

2. The boundaries of the "community" of a total institution as depicted by Goffman are set by the formal organization running it. This view of a total institution as a hybrid between community and bureaucracy does not withstand the scrutiny of comparative research, because social borders of inmates extend well beyond the officially delineated demarcation lines.

3. Such assumptions are implicitly or explicitly at the heart of many approaches to ethnicity. See, for example, Barth (1969) and Geertz (1963).

4. An example of such deliberations can be found in Musgrove (1977), whose discussion touches upon factors of social marginality, the quest for identity and lack of social structure as predictors of the formation of "communes."

5. Suttles employs the term "community of limited liability," which indicates the partial scope in one's life occupied by sponsored communities. This reserved concept of community is useful for our analysis, because it represents a compromise between a totalistic view of the phenomenon and a recognition of is limitation.

6. The Israeli *kibbutzim* and *moshavim* (agricultural settlements) constitute a case in point. For the former, see, for example, Shepher (1980), whose analysis is directly relevant to our discussion; for the latter, see, for example, Weingrod (1966) or Shokeid (1971). In both instances, evolving organizational structure interplays with communal ideologies and shared sentiments to engender the main problems of those realities.

7.   Notwithstanding the criticism often leveled at the analytic usefulness of symbolism in sociocultural anthropology (see, for example, Goody 1977), the predominance of the subject as a central issue in the understanding of behavior cannot be overstated. Rather than giving short shrift to cultural substance, the following sources can be consulted for discussion of the topic, and particularly, the relationship between signified and signifier: Leach (1976), Skorupski (1976), Augé (1982) and Geertz (1973). Geertz offers a relatively dynamic approach to the dialectics between meaning and symbol and, hence is less problematic to our analysis than the others.

8.   This is generally valid, with the semiotic/semiological paradigm being an exception (see, for example, Barthes 1977).

Chapter II

The Ecological Dilemma: Community Versus Residents

The intricacy of the question of boundaries is a manifestation of a broader and more general problem faced by the ethnographer striving for a holistic multifaceted understanding of a "neighborhood" setting. This is the task of making sense of fragmented observations and encounters leading in different directions and having no uniting theme except for the partly haphazard presence of the anthropologist who endeavors to find his bearings under the barrage of information to which he or she is exposed.

What might seem to be purely a methodological issue reserved only for the cognizant, and hence of no concern to the lay reader, is truly a subject of prime importance to the development of any analytic perspective on the neighborhood. The rather amorphic nature of the field, coupled with the need to focus attention and interest on matters related to the operation of Project Renewal within a specific context, goads the researcher into a position of compromise between the exigencies of fieldwork and the quest for meaningful terms of reference within which the data can make sense. The result is an ongoing relationship between observations and their interpretation vis-à-vis the backdrop of locally spun ideas of "community," "urban renewal," "resident participation" and "bureaucratic intervention." The desire to offer an explanation that will do justice to the understanding of both residents under study and matters concerning the operation of Project Renewal in the neighborhood hinges on the assumption that these two objectives are inseparable. It is, indeed, the dyadic interaction between bureaucratically defined neighborhood and the social lives of residents that engenders the predicament of setting community boundaries.

To begin, the concept of neighborhood, which is so deeply entrenched in the very idea of Project Renewal and is so rigidly defined and delineated, could prove to be irrelevant as well as misleading in developing an impartial research approach for the understanding of such a setting. Although the residents assignated as the incuments of a certain Project-sponsored "neighborhood" project reside within a given set of geographical boundaries, it is by no means clear that that area, and the other people within it, are the capsule of their existence. Indeed, it would be a grave misconception to conceive of a neighborhood[1] as an insular environment and to presuppose that that milieu is the hub of its inhabitants' life.

The relative importance of the neighborhood for residents varies a great deal not only among different residents but, more significantly, also from one situation to another. Thus, a resident might find the neighborhood utterly irrelevant to his working life and his employment prospects and at the same time concern himself with his living conditions and his children's education as part and parcel of his immediate surroundings. Whether that surrounding is perceived in the form of a "neighborhood," takes the shape of "urban life," or is molded into an individualistic highly personalized worldview—is all a matter of differential circumstances and various constructions of reality.

Notwithstanding the importance of such a distinction between residents and neighborhood, it should be noted that being under the jurisdiction of a complex administration such as Project Renewal introduces new rules of conduct and novel channels of communication and influence into a neighborhood. The residents of a well-defined territory are thus exposed to and confronted with a myriad of unfamiliar resources, situations, modes of operation and organizational structures. All this is infused into a set of partly old, partly newly-acquired bureaucratic arrangements and, in any case, a rather perplexing system of power and access to authority. Opportunities for initiative and enterprise alongside constraints and limitations make for the emergence of an unstructured, labile socioeconomic context within which a resident might be able to explore new avenues of self-expression in the pursuit of his interests as well as experience confusion and frustration in the face of an unknown and uncertain set-up. All those aspects of life in a Project Renewal controlled area must be taken into due consideration while reckoning with the problem of neighborhood boundaries versus residents' lives, for it is the presence of these factors, however external and even alien to the pre-Project social fabric of the locality they might seem, that renders the setting unique in comparison with other places not administered by the project. This leads to the question of the manner by which a portrait of Arod as a neighborhood may be obtained.

"Hard facts" and irrefutable figures appear to sketch out an unblurred, well-defined profile of the neighborhood. Indeed, it has become a habitual procedure in committee meetings and other official gatherings to produce such "solid" data as seemingly unequivocal evidence to corroborate one point of view or another. However, it has been the case on many such occasions, while the validity of the facts presented was beyond dispute, that meanings and interpretations accorded to them varied considerably. Such observation is almost self-evident, but its importance in shaping the character of this presentation looms beyond the settings of boardrooms and formal agendas. It helps highlight a major issue in the understanding of the neighborhood and, indeed, in the interpretation of any social context.

To put it succinctly, the contention is that the problem of the objective validity of what is regarded as hard-core data is less significant than the usages and implementations of such materials to create, project and manipulate images of reality. This assertion is by no means intended to discount the relevance of censuses, surveys and other sources of context-free information; it merely suggests that such information should be put into perspective and withstand the scrutiny of the analysis of situational conditioning. There are infinite ways of bringing into relief the reality of social life in Arod, and the role of Project Renewal in it, and there is no way of giving short shrift to such substance.

It would be a reassuring presupposition to assume that a multidimensional analysis on different levels of social reality could provide a composite, coherent portrait of life in the neighborhood.

However, field experience has demonstrated that not only is it unconvincing and artificially contrived to present such a picture, but the material obtained does not attest to such a conjecture. The belief that by invoking "reliable" sources of information one is likely to attain a credibly congruous account of the neighborhood is ungrounded in the field because contradictions, discords and disagreement even as to the interpretation of the most basic attributes of the nature and the character of Arod were the rule rather than the exception. Although, as indicated before, there was some common ground of a shared symbolic linguistic-conceptual code, it only served as an accepted umbrella for diverse views and conflicting interests.

The researcher, while watching his step and treading gingerly between the various protagonists and bystanders, is not confronted so much with the problem of taking a stand or a side, but with the delicate role of disentangling the shapeless mass of views, images and actions. Because contrary to a popular maxim, the field does not speak for itself, the researcher is bound, if his account is to be an intelligible one, to speak as it were, for the field by designing a mosaic of data which will imbue the reality under study with meaning.

I. TERRITORY AND INHABITANTS

The Arod neighborhood seems to lend itself to a multiplexity of perspectives, for there is not a single striking feature that could give it a monochrome impression. This is to say that relative to other neighborhoods of similar socioeconomic profile, Arod cannot be regarded as particularly impoverished, exceptionally dilapidated or singularly crime-striken. Furthermore, the heterogeneity of architectural styles—from small ramshackle detached houses, through shabby-looking blocks of flats to modern villas—alongside the multiethnic character of the local population make for a general observation of nonuniformity. However superficial this generalization might seem, it nevertheless has far-reaching implications for the understanding of the search of community symbolism and the quest of "solidarity" and shared commonalities. This part of the residents' behavior will be discussed later. This section concentrates on the background against which such an attribute is formed and generated.

Before touching on matters of socioeconomic importance, the neighborhood has to be located within coordinates of time and space, for these dimensions, no less than others, contribute a great deal toward the visible and invisible boundaries as perceived by the inhabitants.

Arod is one of Netanya's[2] thirty-two boroughs. Like many other "deprived" localities in Israel, it is the outgrowth of a residence inhabited by *Ma'abara* (the transition camps for new immigrants in the early 1950s) evacuees. Having had a nucleus population of Yemenite origin, Arod absorbed two main waves of immigrants. The first, in the mid-1950s, was composed of Ma'abara evacuees of various countries of origin; the second consisted of mainly single or childless couples of Eastern European origin who settled in the area in the early 1970s. These basic demographic parameters constitute the general frame of reference within which the human character and the history of the neighborhood are viewed at present.

Although residents' reconstruction of the past varies a great deal, they are all reluctant to impart ethnic identity or indeed any other common denominator to the neighborhood. Some of them even go as far as stating or implying that Arod is merely a "borough" without any signifying distinct characteristics. Attempts to evoke a sense of unity and solidarity based on common cultural heritage of shared history of immigration does not meet with much success, not only in the neighborhood at large, but also within certain ethnically identifiable groups in it. Ethnic heritage or the legacy of life in the Ma'abara are not regarded as viable links to the present, and an attempt to publish a booklet of local history containing personal life stories, ethnic memorabilia and genealogical family trees was aborted by lack of cooperation on the part of the residents. This state of affairs considerably facilitates the persistent efforts of Project Renewal organizers to engender a locally anchored historical perspective that focuses almost exclusively on the operation of the project. Thus the "preproject" time that was distinguished from "project phase" is marked by apathy, indifference, lack of concern and community care and generaly disarray—adversities that should be rectified and made to disappear with the advent of the project. To signify that trend, the future-oriented term "renewal" is extensively and emphatically used instead of the negatively-charged, past-biased "rehabilitation."

In a newspaper interview, the director of the Project describes the metamorphosis as follows:

> Before the Project Renewal days, we simply couldn't deal with the social problems in the community…. The residents see dramatic changes. They were literally stuck with nothing for 30 years; now they are a part of the aims and goals of the community's renewal. I'd go as far as to say that very soon Arod will be unrecognizable. We are solving the social problems. Employment and transportation are good. We are well-situated between Netanya and Tel-Aviv. The day is not far off when Arod will become a part of the larger Netanya metropolis (Walsh 1982, p. 30).

The desire to be assimilated into the metropolis, epitomizes the double-bind situation with which community-oriented residents and staff members are faced. The transformation from a neglected, down-trodden enclave of poverty and shame into a proud "positive" community is deemed to go through a treadmill of self-effaciveness and obliteration of the past. Thus the objective of becoming an accepted part of the town, rather than being a means to an end, turns into an end in its own right. Under such circumstances, the ultimate goal of creating a "community" with its own distinct identity is self-subversive. Furthermore, as we shall see, the impetus behind assimilation does not derive only from problems of identity and self-esteem, but is largely reinforced by the opportunity to gain political power within the local municipal authority through the presentation of Arod as a "healthy" community, a force to be reckoned with.

The contrast between "before" and "after" is so pronounced that both residents and Project operators contemplated a change in the name of the neighborhood not only as a means of erasing stigmatic smears, but mainly to indicate that a completely new structure had emerged. The symbolically-laden concept of "renewal" evoked a whole galaxy of linguistic cultural associations such as "conversation," "rebirth" and "penitence." Given the religious background of the great majority of residents and considering the incorporation of religious activities and institutions into the operation of the project (see Chapter III), such connotations should not be regarded as exceptional whimsical expressions, but rather as reflections of symbolic codes widely prevalent among residents.

What seems to be a successful enterprise of introducing Project Renewal through commonly accepted cultural channels is really a double-edged sword, for it draws on another aspect of the neighborhood that can be construed as detrimental to the project. This is the fact that neither residents nor project staff can maintain or reproduce a recognized tangible design for neighborhood identity. This, in turn, is probably the main factor responsible for the instant ungullible acceptance of "community" to serve as such a construct. Among the manifold factors responsible for this lack of common ground, it is important to note a few, of which perhaps the most obvious, even though probably the least significant, is the ethnic heterogeneity of the population.

Places of origin cited by residents add up to thirty-two countries scattered around the globe. About one-third of the present population is Israeli-born, whereas the rest are: Moroccan (about 15%); Libyan-Tunisian (around 15%); Yemenite (about 8%); Iraqi (6%); Russian (4.5%); Rumanian (4%); the rest are distributed among two dozen other countries. Although there is a certain correspondence between territorial concentration of specific ethnic categories and residential localities within the neighborhood, with the exception of the veteran Yemenite-identified quarter ("Old Arod"), this is of a very limited consequence of the formation of networks of loyalties, mutual obligations and political allegiance. This is due to the predominant presence of other diversifying factors whose influence overrides the overestimated importance commonly attached to the ethnic divisions.

Residing in Arod, with few exceptions, means that employment is invariably sought outside the neighborhood; therefore, social relationships with workmates are usually based in other areas. Working men more than working women tend to rely on the connection with their trades and occupations, and thus view the network of kins and neighbors as less important than the image attributed to such ties by community workers and welfare staff. Although it appears that in their semiskilled, sometimes manual, occupations there is not much scope for a great scale of variations in earned income, places of work are scattered across a wide area.

In this respect neither daily contact nor mutual interests exist to provide an extended neighborhood association.

The disparity of employment is reinforced by the highly efficient and reliable public transport system that connects Arod to both other districts of Netanya and other towns, of which the most notable is Tel-Aviv. This bus service makes for an easy access to and from the area and compensates, to a large extent, for the relatively small number of privately owned cars. This should be added to the fact that the neighborhood is within a reasonable walking distance from Netanya proper. Thus, an uninhabited area separating Arod from the main town, rather than hampering practical communication with it, serves as a symbolic barrier indicating the sense of isolation and segregation so acutely felt and so meticulously nurtured by residents and project staff.

It should be noted, however, that this physical divide borders only the eastern and the northern sides of the neighborhood. The other two sides, especially the southern border, are delineated by densely inhabited high-rise buildings whose residents identify themselves, and indeed are regarded by the people of Arod, as "middle class." Most of them are Israeli-born or new immigrants from noneastern countries who came to settle in the vicinity in the late 1970s. The visible demarcation line between that residential area and Arod is an ambivalent one, because the attitude expressed toward it by Arod residents is a mixture of avoidance and fascination. Many of them view it as a frontier zone that should be crossed and conquered on the road to realize their middle-class aspirations (see Chapter III). On the other hand, not having reached that desired stage yet, residents refrain from associating themselves, at least publicly, with their neighbors. A tint of guilt or even betrayal on the part of better-off residents "who made it" used to be attached to such ambivalent familiarity. Such is, for instance, the feeling conveyed by a local taxi-driver who has the financial means to move out. Being pressured by his teenage children to take such a step, he expresses his predicament, "I wish I could live in one of those comfortable flats in the skyscrapers on the other side of the road and leave my soul and heart among my friends and family in Arod." This delicately balanced stance reflects some of the problems faced by residents regarding their attitude toward being "in" or "out" of the neighborhood. The patterns of behavior generated by codes of exclusion and inclusion are discussed later (Chapters III and V), but the demographic and socioeconomic basis for the formation of such codes constitutes the following profile of the local population as obtained from data gathered and processed by the information unit of the project (see below), updated through May 1982.

The overall number of the present (1982) population is 6,200 compared to 6,600 in 1972. This drop in population size, caused by young families and post army-service youngsters leaving the neighborhood, is accompanied by a corresponding drop in the size of household units, from 4.7 persons in 1972, to 3.74 in 1982. The number of households, however, has risen by 5 percent. This indicates that the per capita income has risen and that density of housing conditions has decreased over time. The decline in the number of residents has altered the age structure of the neighborhood, making it into a proportionately aging area with 13 percent of its population being over the age of 60. This increase accounts for the growing load of welfare cases among the higher age groups and for the preoccupation with community services for the aged, as well as for the concern expressed by many residents regarding the "demographic imbalance" in the neighborhood. The most significantly marked age categories are 0-17 (37%); 18-59 (50%); and 60+ (13%).

What is markedly telling about the above data is not so much the actual figures but the manner in which age-group composition is arranged. Until the age of 21 people are assumed to have their lives organized and monitored according to age-related and age-bound social institutions—nursery, compulsory kindergarten, primary school, high school, and the army for ages 0-3, 4-5, 6-14, 15-17, 18-21, respectively. However, once such age-oriented institutions cease to predominate one's life, the division between age-grades is devised arbitrarily.

This observation, which might seem too general and too self-evident to be addressed specifically to Arod, bears out a significant characteristic of the operation of the project in the neighborhood, because most of the activities and frameworks it offers are based on such perceived age-set roles, assignment of task teams, and appeals to the public are formulated and allocated to correspond with this age-structure. The significance of this fact rests with its

Table II.1. Distribution of Age Groups in Arod

	Age	Persons	Percentage
1	0-3	319	5.7
2	4-5	250	4.5
3	6-14	973	17.5
4	15-17	349	6.3
5	18-21	470	8.5
6	22-34	1112	21.5
7	35-44	429	7.0
8	45-54	461	8.3
9	55-64	469	8.5
10	65+	476	8.6
			100

being an indication of an attempt to overlook other conceivable criteria of dividing the population into designated groups for functions carried out by the project. Rather than fostering and cultivating existing locally entrenched and established divisions, the project resorts to a neutral form of restructuring the neighborhood, thus avoiding interference with the locally-based alleged divisions, and hence receiving wide cooperation and support for its policies.

The most commonly accepted internal division was that of "Old Arod," "New Arod" and "Arod Kablanim V'yavne," termed A, B and C, respectively. All of the three are geographically defined residential areas of locally perceived distinctly different socioeconomic and political characteristics. Indeed, most of the local disputes and claims for power and influence revolved around the three vicinities. Arod A is populated mainly by the neighborhood veterans of Yemenite origin who were the first settlers in the area who, besides claims for rights of seniority, regard themselves as the long-established heart of the "community." This advocacy for a privileged position is reinforced by the relatively high degree of involvement in local affairs that has marked the residents of Arod A during the years. In private conversation and nonofficial utterances, many residents of Arod A maintained that the record of the area in criminal activities and welfare cases is low in comparison with other parts of the neighborhood, investing them with a special status of setting an example for the rest and leading the way toward renewal. Such arguments of "quality" are punctuated by the fact that the population of Arod A is dwindling rapidly and in 1982 comprised 27 percent of the total population of the neighborhood.

The threat to the traditionally-held power base of Arod A precipitates some of the old established stalwarts of that residence to prevaricate the process of electing a new neighborhood committee and to employ absenteeism and other impeding stratagems to foil any attempt to form an officially recognized different constellation of local forces. The main challenge that induced this maneuvering came from residents of Arod B, which comprised 51 percent of the total population. These are mainly Israeli born, second generation residents of north African origin whose economic state has improved considerably in recent years, and who, consequently, consider themselves as having experienced political "awakening." Indeed, most of the activities in the project's operation belong to that category of residents. This "awakening" occurred because of the malfunctioning of the elected political organs of the neighborhood. The project remained unsupervised by local representation, and thus accessible to all manners and forms of solicited and unsolicited involvements. For a while the project was treated as an arena free of locally established influences and intrigues, thus enabling and even encouraging the emergence of new political opportunities and entrepreneurs.

The project as a breeding ground for the rise of new local leadership is discussed at some length in Chapter IV. For the purpose of this description, suffice it to say that the power struggle generated by that set of circumstances does not involve residents of Arod C, for they are thought to be the weakest sector in the neighborhood, consisting of welfare cases, the aged and single parent households. Low income, dependence on welfare services, lack of family support networks and poor housing are the main characteristics that constitute the face of that area. It is for this reason that Arod C is frequently a target for social workers' interest and serves as a symbol of deprivation and neglect whenever the cause of the weak and the poor has to be invoked as one of the justifications for the operation of Project Renewal and the necessity of a "healthy community" being created. However, that population has never been addressed as potential initiators and organizers of "community" spirit, but rather as mere recipients of and passive participants in such work.

The attitude expressed toward Arod C demonstrates one of the major dilemmas faced by residents of a Project Renewal neighborhood. This is the intractable predicament of being regarded as "deprived," "dependent" and "backwards," on the one hand, and aiming for "independence," "self-sufficiency" and "pride," on the other. This contradiction is the main subject of Chapter IV, but it does draw on one of the main concerns of the current discussion.

II. PEOPLE AND "PROBLEMS"

A few issues are traditionally and officially set to represent the main indicators of deprivation. Rate of crime—chiefly drug offenses, vandalism, prostitution, theft, and robbery—poor housing conditions, inferior standard of education and rate of unemployment seem to offer the most commonly accepted parameters for assessing extent of deprivation. Therefore, it is instructive to gain some insight into the meanings ascribed to deprivation by Arod's residents.

Crime has been alleged to be on the decline for the last three years and, in any case, in the absence of conclusive police records, crimes committed in the neighborhood are usually attributed to outsiders who give Arod its "bad name." Most of the residents who address the subject deny any anxiety or fear connected with their own physical safety. This, as is shown in Chapter III, is in sharp contrast with the image of a violent and hazardous area depicted by the project staff. Although such a denial of the existence of violence in the neighborhood must not be taken as an objective assessment of the situation and not even as a genuine account of what residents feel and fear, it should be noted that to a certain extent it is attested to by the reluctance of residents to take any safety precautions in the form of security arrangements, such as participating in the ranks of the local civil guard or demanding more extensive police patroling. Unemployment, poor education and deprived living conditions are rarely mentioned as possible causes for criminal behavior.

Unemployment is indeed a subject under constant dispute in the neighborhood. Different surveys produced different figures and thus make it impossible to denote a credible record of unemployment. In a door-to-door survey conducted by the information unit of the project, the following data was obtained:

1509	employed residents
220	registered unemployed residents
35	school dropouts (before conscription)
1764	Total (= 32.5% of the employable population)

The rest of the population consists of housewives, regular soldiers, school students, the sick, the disabled and old-age pensioners (see Table II.2). However, an unemployment officer appointed by the project maintains that official records supported by information obtained locally suggests that the rate of unemployment in Arod does not exceed 5 percent of the local work force.

The reason for this discrepancy is not necessarily a flaw in the method of investigation nor is it due to unreliable sources; rather, it rests with the different sets of interests guiding the gleaning and processing of the data. While the first survey was conducted by a team whose main concern was to set unemployment as a target for extensive community work, the second assessment was made by a worker whose conception of the neighborhood was one of full employment with only a marginal problem of "unemployable" residents. Indeed, many of the residents concurred with this evaluation by stressing the view that those who are out of work are so because of some fault of their one, and not because of forces of circumstance. Thus, those who subscribe to such an approach equate unemployment with unemployability and rule out any possibility of changing the situtation by training schemes, personal encouragement, occupational counselling, or, in the long run, through education.

This seemingly fatalistic attitude is reflected in various walks of life and particularly in the area of education. Although residents reiterate the great importance they attach to the role of good education in the advancement of themselves and their children, outsiders to the neighborhood and particularly welfare workers are baffled by what they termed "apathy" or "lack of interest" shown

Table II.2. Distribution of Unemployed According to Age

Age	Number of Unemployed
14-17	17
18-21	38
22-30	97
31-44	19
45-60	15
61+	1
age unknown	33
Total	220

by parents toward the schooling of their children. This is assumed to be corroborated by the unwillingness of parents to involve themselves in school activities, or to participate in devising their children's curriculum—a provision that is made available to parents under Ministry of Education regulations. Appeals by social workers to parents to develop school committee meetings into a basis of community work are met with unenthusiastic response, as are attempts to heighten their awareness of the potential of good schooling for children's careers and life prospects.

Typical of this is the satisfaction expressed by most parents with the whole educational system and particularly with the schools serving the neighborhood. There are few complaints about the adequacy of facilities, state of equipment, standard of teaching and efficiency of management. Nor are any suggestions broached regarding subject matter, teaching methods and extra-school curricula.

When asked about educational and professional aspirations for their children, many parents, particularly those occupying the lower echelons of the local economic pyramid, argue, as one mother stated that "now that we are an organized neighborhood, the community can take good care of our children." Another parent, whose four sons attend a local primary school, insists that "their future is secure in the hands of the Project. They know what education is all about." The motif of according "community" the fostering role of educational care-taker and future guardian also permeates street corner gossip, morning encounters of housewives and husbands' daily small talk during bus rides to and from work:

Table II.3. Synagogue Distribution According to Ethnic Group

Country of Origin	Number of Synagogues
Yemen	9
Morocco	4
Libya	3
Iraq	2
Ashkenazi[4]	1
Persia	1
Georgia	1
Nonethnic	1
Total	22

"If it were not for Begin,[3] Gods bless his soul, and the Project and all the good people from America, my children wouldn't have had a chance in life. They would have been like wild animals without a community and without self-respect."

An example of activity that seems to dispute the assumption of apathy and indifference is the proliferation of synagogues in the neighborhood[5] (see Table II.3). Although most of Arod's residents declare themselves to be "religious," only a few congregate for daily service, and those who do are mainly elderly. In fact, the major functions of the synagogues during weekdays is to serve as a venue for social gatherings. A more extensive reference to the religious life in Arod is made in Chapter III. It should be noted, however, that despite the relatively high number of synagogues in the area, they are not used as power bases for recruiting political support and that the multiethnic mosaic of religious affiliations does not reflect local factionalism.

Moreover, being aware of the threat that reorganization of the neighborhood by the project might pose to congregants' involvements—both in participation and donation—in synagogues, many religious leaders avoid any confrontation with the newly-emergent neighborhood institutions. Thus, a distinction is often made between, as one local Rabbi put it, "Congregation (*Edah*) and community (*Kehilah*)[6]—the first belongs to God and the second to the government." Cooperation is sought in areas of overlapping activities dictated by unavoidable occasions, such as

festivals and public events of religious connotation (the *Mimuna*—
see Chapter III).

Most religious functionaries asserted that their contentment
with the current situation is unreserved and that their only fear
does not rest with official intervention, but with growing
"secularity" among the younger generation, whose religious
commitment in the form of synagogue attendance and observing
the Sabbath, and so forth, was waning.

An area where immediate improvement is regarded in the
neighborhood as highly beneficial, both at present and in terms
of future plans, is the area of housing. Here, unlike in
unemployment and education, residents do show initiative and
resourcefulness in approaching the authorities, making claims,
criticizing, and expecting action. Invariably, residents complain
about the lack of assistance they received in the form of mortgages
and refurbishing, compared with that enjoyed by their neighbors.
Yet such grievances are not voiced publicly and never reach the
stage of active protest. Awareness of the role of the physical project
in local renovation work is at a very general level and does not
exceed some vague knowledge, including the name of the project
manager and the location of the project's offices. Indeed, most of
the residents who consider themselves to be in need of improving
their housing conditions lay the responsibility for doing this on
Amidar (the pre-project public housing agency) and consequently,
approach the local office with any query or demand regarding the
state of their residence.

This trend should be understood against the background of the
fact that 51 percent of the 1,640 occupied residential units in Arod
are rented tenancies from Amidar. These flats and houses have a
purchase option that many residents want to realize, especially in
view of the rising market value of property in the area. Thus,
residents believe that their prime concern should be with the
bureaucracy of Amidar rather than with any other official agency.
Occasionally though, some of them ask Project Renewal staff or
municipal social workers to facilitate contact with Amidar
officials, but the rigid division of functions between the two
authorities is keenly preserved and sustained.

Two main categories of grounds for improved housing
conditions are employed by residents. The first concerns claims

made by handicapped or elderly residents, who, because of difficulties in mobility and problems of dampness and squalor, find their accommodations unsuitable. The second basis for rehousing is family size, particularly the number of children.

With the decline in the population of the neighborhood, and especially, the decreasing proportion of young families, the number of households with more than three or four children has also dropped. This state of affairs engenders a division of views and interests between two schools of social organizers. While the welfare staff and the social work-oriented community workers maintain that Arod is still an area of a considerable number of "children-blessed" families—the officially-used Israeli euphemism for families with many children—Project Renewal and many residents belittle that alleged characteristic of the neighborhood. What seems to be a difference of opinion is really a reflection of a cleavage in the basic conception of the desirable image of the neighborhood vis-à-vis interests and preconceptions. This is a conflict between treating the neighborhood first and foremost as an aggregate of problems amenable to work by social workers, or alternatively, viewing it as a "normal" community on the road to the realization of the Israeli stereotype of middle-class urban suburbia (see discussion in Chapter III).

The data regarding such families lend themselves to different interpretations, and thus well serve either party in that dispute. The figures obtained and provided by the information unit are listed in Table II.4.

Because there is some methodological confusion as to the distinction between the concepts "family" and "household," it is not clear whether some domestic units are composed of more than one nuclear family. Although data about the number and size of household units is available, the economic structure of such units is still unclear. The only piece of information to that effect is that out of 1,961 family household units, 51 are double, which presumably means the coexistence of two domestic units inhabiting a residential dwelling. The rest of the data is too incomplete even to suggest a sound criterion of distinction between a kin-based economic unit and a kin-based residence (see Table II.5).

Table II.4. Family Size and Population Distribution

Family Size	Percentage in the Population
1-2 members	38
3-4 members	30
5-6 members	20
7+ members	12

Table II.5. Number of Household Units and Household Size

Number of Household Units		Size of Household
	575	1-2
	733	3-6
	176	7+
Total	1484 (available for interview)	

In view of the dearth of surrounding relevant data it would be presumptuous to accord certain statements, however substantiated by figures, the social significance attributed to them by those who care to produce them. Thus, the fact that 20 percent of the families consists of at least six members is of no consequence to the understanding of the problems incurred by "children-blessed" households, if no supporting information is provided, that is, age composition, work-force, level of income, division of labor, and so on. The same ambiguity applies to another fact, which, on the surface, seems to suggest the prevalence of a "social problem." This is the fact that 22 percent of the household units are headed by women.

Indeed, either interest party brings out "evidence" in support of its perspective in the form of "cases" that fit into its argument. A one-parent family with five children who manages to make ends meet can be set as an example of "nonproblematic" or "normal" living, whereas another family enmeshed in the "cycle of deprivation" with a long record of involvement with welfare agencies represents a typecast for the stereotype of the neighborhood. Because the latter approach focuses on individuals and "case work," whereas the former advocates a "community-oriented" conception, it is important to note the elements in the neighborhood emphasized by either angle.

Poor housing conditions and low incomes are not sufficient causes, in the eyes of the social workers, to account for and to justify dependency on welfare and the need for the provision of welfare services. Poverty is deemed to be a socioculturally generated state of mind just as it is a consequence of economic deprivation. The characteristics of this mental state are deemed to be inability and unwillingness to cope, lack of sense of achievement and competitiveness, and adherence to obsolete traditional values. It all amounts to personal maladaptation and social stagnation. Notwithstanding the origins and the construction of such images in terms of the neighborhood, it can mean that the residents are made up from a set of endemic "social inadequacies" and "pathologies" that can only be cured by education and integration. For the time being, however, the only available palliative is the sinecure of welfare supported by the restricted contribution of the individual. Therefore, the individual is both the cause of and the target for outside intervention.

A seemingly diametrically opposite view is held by those for whom the individual can be overriden by the "community." This conviction does not disagree with the syndrome of individual ailments diagnosed by social workers, but holds that by submerging the individual into a greater whole, meaning, the "community," his personal problems will be resolved or erased, for he will go through a process of regeneration and reidentification. This conception of "community" as a panacea for deprivation and its implication is discussed later. For the purpose of this section, however, I shall concentrate on the institutions, establishments and forms of social organization that make for the recognized identity of Arod as a "community" at work. A detailed mapping of such facilities and functions is outlined following an introduction that sketches the structure of the various organizations, official bodies and agencies operating in the neighborhood, which constitute the outer tangible layer of the local "community," and form its visible contours.

It should be noted, however, that the following do not have any necessary bearings on residents' awareness of their existence, nor do they imply contents and aims of activities. In fact, for the purpose of the current discussion, they are merely a conglomerate of readily localized self-declared centers designated for selected public gatherings.

III. THE "COMMUNITY"

A cursory survey of the Arod neighborhood readily locates an abundance of premises designated for some public function. Some of them serve more than one purpose and are frequented by alternating groups of residents. With the exception of strictly defined establishments such as synagogues, kindergartens and health services, most other publicly-owned buildings have flexible schedules and accommodate different functions. Recently, local schools have followed suit and have begun to offer their facilities for extra-curricular activities in the afternoon and evenings. The "WIZO" (World Zionist Organization) women's federation runs a social club, which is the only leisure-oriented facility not officially connected with the project. Other public services include the local branch of the Histadrut trade union-controlled sick fund and two Amidar housing offices. Although most of the other contacts with government officials have to be made in Netanya proper, a few representatives of certain agencies come to the neighborhood on a regular basis to attend to residents, such as the counselling service for the aged, which belongs to the National Insurance and also the welfare workers of the Netanya municipality, who hold regular and frequent reception hours in Arod.

The Matnas (Hebrew acronym for Center of Culture, Youth and Sport) of Arod is the hub of "community" life and the organizational, bureaucratic, territorial and symbolic center for all the activities, schemes and values revolving around the idea of Project Renewal as the dominant regenerating force in the neighborhood. The range of activities organized and run by the Matnas is broad and varied and will be specified below. The sites wherein these activities take place are also numerous and are scattered all around the neighborhood. There are six public air raid shelters that have been redesignated and redesigned to accommodate social functions. There are two flats, one serving as a social club for the aged and the other as offices for community work. There is a large building with facilities for sports, public gatherings and other recreational activities. Extensive use is made of available local premises such as schools, parks, halls and other public and even privately owned utilities, such as sheds in backyards to store tools and cleaning materials, and kitchens to prepare food for public events. It should be noted, however, that the use of such private facilities is selective and is confined to amenities owned by workers, paid or voluntary, of the project, thus attesting to their involvement with the activities.

The temporary headquarters of the Matnas is in a renovated community center, which consists of the main offices, a boardroom and a library. The building, located at the heart of Arod, is easily accessible and is regarded as a recognized focal point of the neighborhood. In anticipation of the inauguration of the permanent Matnas, or as some of Arod's residents prefer to call it, the "country club"—a symbolic anticipatory acquisition of middle-class identity, the present premises is viewed as merely a necessary transitional stage, which accounts for its modest size and the limited range of facilities it offers. It is important to note that no contact whatsoever has been established between the social project and the physical one. Both bodies try their best to avoid trespassing and to remain mutually exclusive in operation and ambition. Extra precaution is taken not to advise residents on matters relating to the other aspect of the project and not a tint of criticism can be detected in references concerning either agency.

The centrality of the Matnas in the neighborhood is very much shaped and determined by the organizational set-up of its operation. The Matnas is made to combine and govern all the activities and functions undertaken by the social project, and its administration is designed to carry out the objectives set by the project director. The distribution of power among Matnas staff does not necessarily reflect the formal role structure and the assignments devised and formulated by the authorities. The real division of labor is an ever-changing consequence of a complex set of relationships based on varying interests, changing boundaries and different resources. Conflicts, strifes, alliances and collaborations compose the everyday political reality of the projects, and strategies of all kinds are employed to contrive the construction of events and images to establish a fit between interests and resources. Self-evident as this might seem, it nevertheless needs reminding both to serve as a preamble to the ensuing analysis and as a preventative reservation to precede the following description of the formal structure of the project in Arod.

Perhaps the most significant characteristic of the Arod project rests with the merger of the two predominant "community" oriented roles, that of the head of the local community center, the Matnas, and that of the director of the local Project Renewal. The fusion of the two functions into one provides the basis for centrality of decision making and for considerable personal authority controlled by the incumbent of that joint position. The fact that in the case of Arod that person is also a residential living in the neighborhood, added another intricate dimension to the performance of the role and to the self-image and the social conception surrounding it. The built-in contradiction and the seeming ambivalence embedded in such a combination make for ample grounds for public controversy on the one hand, and a broad latitude for manipulation on the other.

A deputy director, a nonresident, was appointed in November 1982 to discharge the administrative operation of the project, thus enabling the director to allocate more time for assuming further responsibilities regarding matters of policymaking and direct personal involvement in local affairs. This proved to be of great benefit to the director during the preparation for the local election of the neighborhood committee.

The lower echelon of project staff consists of 6 or 7 coordinators of designated social activities such as sport, culture, "problematic" youth, adult education, the aged, mothers' training scheme, and the local youth movement. Other workers of the project include full-time and part-time instructors, office staff and maintenance staff. A topical issue in staff meetings used to be the dispute over the proportion of local employees versus nonresident workers running the project. The argument remains unabated and the conflict unresolved even in the light of the indisputable facts and figures produced by both parties. This is because although nobody has grounds to discount the number of local project employees cited by the director, there still exists a poignant disagreement as to the kind of assignments and the amount of power imparted to residents' staff. It is worth noting that neither age, professional experience, sex or ethnic origin creates similar divisions. Chapter V explicates the reasons for this phenomenon by grounding it in conceptions of community vis-à-vis temporal orientations. It is argued that the ephemerality of the project renders all the above categories insignificant compared to the distinction between belonging permanently to the neighborhood, that is, being a resident, and flitting through it, that is, being just a staff member.

Tension concerning the subject of residents' involvement in the project intensifies when members of the team of community and welfare workers join the Matnas staff in joint project meetings, with the former advocating stronger grass-roots participation and power-sharing with residents and the latter expressing "professional" reservations as to the competence and the ability of residents to assume such responsibilities.

The organization of the project as a professional body governed by residents and executing their will, follows almost to the letter the pattern prescribed by the central bureaucratic authorities of the national project. Members of staff share a heightened awareness of the rules and regulations that constitute the administrative framework of the project and usually take great pains to adhere to the code of convening committees regularly, submitting reports on time and following the protocol procedures without fail. They are also assiduously careful to show open-mindedness through seeking advice and counselling from whoever is in an official position to offer it.

However, what might seem to be an almost ritualistic performance of a bureaucratic practice serves a distinct function running the project. It is often emphasized by the director and his aides that following red tape requirements, perfunctory though as it appears to be, facilitates communication with the central authorities of the project. In the absence of informal channels of influence with those bodies (see Chapter IV), adherence to unequivocally formulated rules of conduct is deemed to be both a framework for expected "good management" and a safeguard against political criticism. The inability to negotiate terms with the authorities is thus manifested in restoring to structure, rather than to content, as the former is evidently unarguable while the latter can be easily contested. To quote one of the workers who assisted with the completion of some forms in recording activities and their respective budget allocation, "It doesn't matter what you write as long as the rubrics look black."

Thus, the management of contacts with officials and authorities are meticulously handled to meet the most particular requirements, especially in the area of funding arrangements and budget planning and accounting. This attitude is also reflected in the immaculate hospitality extended to visitors and in the high importance placed on public image and public relations. Even children behave as if such concerns are their responsibility. Visitors to the neighborhood were showered with offers of assistance and guidance and those with "official" appearance or "tourist" image are instantly escorted by groups of children who volunteer unsolicited information regarding the location of the Matnas and the whereabouts of its workers. It is not uncommon to see children minding the office or laboring over minor chores in public premises. Such involvement is encouraged and, to some extent, induced by members of staff who regard it as evidence of the rising community spirit.

As is shown in Chapter IV, the project endeavors to maintain an image of autonomy and independence. This is projected into positions taken regarding the main life-line of the Arod project. Thus the role of government agencies is consistently belittled, whereas the contribution of the Jewish Agency, the association of Matnases and the sister community in New Jersey are considered to be important and are amplified accordingly in both external and internal communications. In fact, most of the residents are unaware of the complex system of government agencies that are involved in administering the project, and the full credit for the new range of resources and services is given to the Jewish Agency and to American Jewry, in particular. A special tribute is often paid to the Prime Minister without much regard to the fact that Mr. Begin, being the head of the state administration, operates through various ministries. Very few residents, for example, are cognizant of the role the Deputy Prime Minister plays in the national project—head of the project and Minister of Housing. This, in spite of the fact that the incumbent of that position at the time of the research was Mr. David Levy, whose background as a Moroccan-born immigrant from a deprived neighborhood made him almost into a living symbol of the hope that Project Renewal had in store in the public eye.

During most of the period in which this study was conducted, the steering committee, as well as the neighborhood committee and the local activists, played a significantly low-key part in affairs and relationships related to the project. The reasons for this are elucidated later (Chapters IV and V), but our understanding of the structure of the project and the manner of its operation cannot be complete without drawing attention to a few aspects of this issue.

Although the introduction of the project into Arod's life has been most welcomed by residents, and even though appreciation and recognition have been abundantly voiced, the residents, on the whole, do not regard the project as the focus of community life, nor do they find it rewarding or beneficial to participate in various programs set up by its staff. The reason for this is simply that most of the residents find the notion of Arod as a community totally unimportant in their daily existence.

This has nothing to do with the "attractiveness," the "efficiency," the "popularity" or even the services of the project. Rather, it draws on the fact that on the one hand, residents do not view and treat Arod as an insular enclave with defined boundaries, and on the other hand, the commonly accepted realization that the institutions, networks of relationships and resources that the project claim to supersede are regarded as either irrelevant or replaceable. This point is discussed throughout the book and particularly in Chapter IV, but it should be generally noted that the tenuous fabric of power relationships in the neighborhood are seen as a boon rather than as a bane, and certainly in no need of bolstering and cultivating. Because most residents consider Arod to be a transitory, albeit not unpleasant, stage in their lives, and as many of them conduct a great deal of their activities outside the neighborhood, the commonplace view is that the project is a temporary, perhaps necessary palliative, but one without any significant bearings on the residents' social and personal future.

This attitude of high praise and expressed satisfaction, on the one hand, and seeming lack of enthusiasm in participation, on the other, make for the emergence of the principal dilemma of Project Renewal in Arod—the apparent ambivalence of an elaborate structure of activities and functions that meet with a paucity of residents' involvement, or as one of the residents put it, "a community without community participation." The resident, not surprisingly, a sociology student, goes on to explain that, "Here in Arod, we need the motivation steered by community spirit, but the community institutions established for us by government 'know-alls' only put it in shackles. This is the reason why these institutions are and will be defunct." In our phrasiology: sentiment without structure, or is it? Accepting community as an ethos while rejecting it as a catch-phrase to justify every scheme subsumed under "urban renewal" or "neighborhood rehabilitation" produces a duality in the meaning of the concept for residents. While the ethos is hailed and aspired for, community institutions are regarded as manifestations of another slogan rather than as expressions of the genuine spirit of the ideal. The social world of community is spun by the former, interwoven into the latter.

As will be argued in Chapter V, conceptions of "community" are variegated in accordance with the sets of interests and ideologies that furnish them. Nevertheless, when ideas of community activity are put into practice and are embodied in diverse forms of public functions, there seems to exist a broad agreement among the perpetrators of such activities regarding the status of an event as a "community" affair or otherwise. The reason for this rests with the common interest shared by all those whose professional preoccupation and justification are enmeshed in propagating the idea of "community" and in proliferating community-oriented frameworks. These members of staff devote a considerable amount of time and resources to initiate, promote, produce and reproduce meetings, gatherings, assignments, projects and schemes aimed at establishing Arod as a neighborhood worthy of earning the title of "a community."

A tour around Arod's public gathering places designed to accommodate community functions reveals an extensive and varied range of activities. A rough distinction can be made between regular activities and one-time events. The question of the responsibility for the organization of activities seems to carry less weight than the visibility and the accessibility of such occurrences. Residents of Arod are unaware of, and indeed are not interested in, the forces behind those functions, and as such activities are aimed at attracting their attention and participation, primary importance should be placed on constructing that reality, rather than on its origins and the impetus behind it.

Members of staff measure their success in boosting community consciousness by the number of new recruits attending the activities organized by them. Thus, wide publicity is given to planned projects and a great deal of concern is expressed regarding the effectiveness and the impact of various ways of approaching the public and getting the information across. Several problems involved in this issue of conveying messages to residents can illuminate several facets of the image of the neighborhood in the eyes of members of staff. On a number of occasions, it was argued that printed material in the form of newsletters, newspapers, billboard advertising, and home-delivered leaflets are "a waste of time and money, since nobody bothers to read them anyway." This attitude is fostered by the alleged illiteracy of most of the residents and the imputed lack of motivation and interest to handle any written material.

Much effort is spent in suggesting alternative media, such as megaphone-delivered public addresses and the use of informal networks of kith and kin to relay information. It is strongly recommended that project staff should employ their contacts with residents in the service of that mission. Thus, the nucleus of residents who attend project functions is made to be a broker of information to the rest of the neighborhood. Needless to say, such an approach is based on a whole set of assumptions, some of which are unfounded preconceptions. It should also be noted that such an operation defeats the very idea of "community" being a product of grass-roots participation, for it outrightly discounts the will and ability of residents to initiate and develop "community" oriented functions. Furthermore, it inherently presupposes an unbridgeable breach between project staff and residents. This is not just a breakdown of communication channels, but primarily a discrepancy in worlds of meaning and terms of reference. To accept such an idea and to act accordingly only means that the whole concept of community creation is a self-denying construct.

The analysis of this breach and its inherent contradiction is valid only if there is convincing evidence to support the implicit premise that the expressed aspiration of project staff to build a "community" is not merely lip service to a professional manifesto, but a consistent effort to state a case and to consolidate it through the conduct of the project.

Evidently such a question cannot and, indeed, should not be answered in clear-cut decisive terms, but the amount of evidence tipping the balance toward the assumption that project staff exerted themselves to institute what they deemed "a community" is plentiful. Far from attempting to assess authenticity of intentions and sincerity of motives, the fact is that the only common language with which activities and plans are discussed and through which decisions and suggestions are rationalized and legitimized is the nomenclature of community. Staff meetings, official records, publicly addressed messages and informal encounters are replete with "community"-related jargon, and the conviction that the creation of community is the ultimate goal of all the work and time invested in the project is made into the cornerstone of any reference to the neighborhood as a target for social intervention. Thus, the problem of establishing a link between the range of activities offered by the project and the lack of satisfactory response from residents is still the key issue for the understanding of the operation of Project Renewal in Arod.

Out of the two aforementioned categories of project functions, the second one—that of one-time events—is the most controversial. The reason for this is rooted in the drain on financial resources incurred by inviting shows and performing artists to visit the neighborhood or by funding subsidized bookings for residents. Trips and tours also prove to be a costly enterprise and doubt has often been cast as to their significance in furthering the cause of "community" awareness. Thus, the coordinators of such events would frequently find themselves in a defensive position regarding the justification versus cost of their propositions. Nevertheless, funds were eventually available and programs of entertainment are seldom curtailed or phased out.

It is convenient to accept the argument of those who oppose such activities that the relative ease of organizing such short-lived projects accounts for their popularity. They maintain that by encouraging one-time events, some of which are lavish, the project gains immediate and impressive visibility at a relatively low cost of investment. Thus, exposing the public to such affairs produces instant results in terms of enjoyment and dependency on the resources and good will of the organizer, but yields no long-term fruit in terms of cultivating a "community."

Although the observation itself might be correct, the reason for the state of affairs it represents should be sought along a different vein of explanation to the one suggesting "laziness" and "convenience." This interpretation, which ramifies from the abovementioned breach in communication between respective conceptions of staff and residents, suggests that most of the policymaking decisions taken by the project are governed by yet another contradiction inherent in the structure of Project Renewal as a whole. This is the time-lag between the declared objectives of the project and the available pool of means and resources with which it offers to attain those objectives, in other words, the overt discrepancy between the long-term goal of creating a "community" and the limited operational period of the project.

Members of staff, whose confidence in the potential and the ability of residents to evolve into "community conscious people" is scant, are fully aware of the time factor involved in their efforts. The brevity of the project and its destined terminality drives members of staff toward targets and achievements within the reach of their time resources. As those resources are uncertain, both in terms of the future of the overall project in Arod and within the personal context of one's employment prospects and career opportunities, there is a growing tendency to rely on what seems to be safe, low risk, visible and recognized accomplishments. The problem of terminality is discussed throughout as having a considerable impact on people's conduct; the case of the handling of one-time events is but one illustration in support of a more general argument that will be developed later.

Notwithstanding the frequency of one-time events in Arod, the regular activities will constitute the main bulk of the project's work. It would be senseless to enumerate a detailed list of weekly activities, for such activities must be understood and examined within the context of their participants and organizers. Such references will be made in Chapters III, IV and V. It is instructive, however, to present a general idea of the extent and the scale of such activities by referring to the official annual 1983-1984 project report submitted to the Inter-Ministerial Committee of Project Renewal (see Table II.6). Although this document concerns itself chiefly with matters pertaining to budget arrangements, funding facilities and the allocation of personnel, it does reflect in great

Table II.6. Project Renewal Annual Report—
Projects and Activities

1. A psychologists' counseling service for infants	14. Post-army youth program
2. Preventative medicine scheme	15. Sports activities—30 groups across the age grades
3. Intensified individual care— a social-work project	16. Scholarships for students
4. Games' club for mothers and their children	17. Local theater company
5. Program for training young mothers	18. Local entertainment group
6. Intensified kindergarten care	19. Visual art workshops
7. Aid to local primary schools— equipment, psychological service and apprenticeship scheme	20. Old-age social club
	21. Individual care for the aged
	22. General welfare services
	23. Arod's information unit
8. Local youth movement	24. Workshop for the care of yards (a euphemism for hygiene and tidiness)
9. Library	
10. Adult education program	25. A school for neighborhood activisits
11. Preparatory course for pre-army youth	
12. Girls in distress	26. Local newspaper
13. Organizing street-corner youth groups	27. Summer schools for children, working mothers and the elderly

accuracy the kind and scope of operations carried out by the project. Evidently, the formal nature of the account disguises behind it a multitude of relevant factors such as conflicts of interests, decision-making processes, and the relationship between content and context of activities. Nevertheless, it is a necessary background for the observations and arguments which will constitute the following chapters.

All of the first 14 items clearly attest to the argument concerning the lack of trust on the part of members of staff in the readiness of Arod's residents to reach the desired goal of creating a "community." They all imply that residents should be guided, supervised and educated from cradle to grave. The principle of this indoctrination is discussed later, but if a "community" is an outgrowth of residents' "maturity," as many members of staff state, the activities to which they are expected to be drawn strongly suggest just the opposite. Rather, an image of the underdeveloped, insecure and helpless resident emerges.

The clear distinction made in the report and, indeed, in most staff meetings and project communications between "welfare activities" and "community frameworks" is designed to separate between the stigma-afflicted resident who is incapable of taking care of his own affairs, let alone creating a "community," and the social organizer who, by being in charge of "community"-oriented programs, constructs the edifice for the would-be Arod community. Thus, while the individual resident is backwards, unprepared and unaware, the collectivity is a problem-free entity that can furnish the fire of "community" life. Obviously, the assumption that the whole is larger than the sum of its parts dominates the position, otherwise such a contradiction could not be ignored. As we see in Chapter V, such convictions serve as a pivotal theme in shaping the image of "community" among project staff.

Perhaps more telling than the list of activities is the budgetary breakdown of those activities, both in terms of the proportional allocation of funds and of the distribution of contributions between the Jewish Agency and the government of Israel. Table II.7, based on the same report, presents both data for the year 1982/1983.

Except for "formal education" (12%), that is, schools, employment (1%) and administration (2.5%)—a total of 15.5 percent of the Arod budget—all the items listed are, in various shapes and forms, community-geared budgets. It is interesting to note that welfare services are bound up to "community development," because the social workers insist on emphasizing that association as a mark of the nature of their work.

Evidently, overlapping is wide and the distinction between various functions and activities is blurred. This allows for a broad leeway of bargaining and interchanging budgetary items. It also indicates the relative freedom of members of staff in deciding frameworks for activities while adhering to the all-embracing definition of "community."

Finally, comment must be made on the proportion of contribution between the Jewish Agency and the Government. Clearly, the greater dependency and, for that matter, expressed loyalty to the Jewish Agency, stems from constraints of budget allocations, rather than moral conviction or social commitment.

Table II.7. Budgetary Breakdown of Community Projects

Item	Percentage of the Budget	Jewish Agency (approx.)	Government (approx.)	Total
Ages 0-5	13	25	75	100
Ages 5+				
Formal education	12	20	80	100
Nonformal education	4	100	0	100
Youth movement	10.5	60	40	100
Sport	5	100	0	100
Adult Education	13	100	0	100
Cultural and social activities	6	100	0	100
The aged	8.5	45	55	100
Welfare and community development	18	33	67	100
Employment	1	100	0	100
Community projects	6.5	90	10	100
Administration	2.5	100	0	100
Total	100			

Nevertheless, irrespective of the reason for greater affiliation to the Jewish Agency, the feeling of dependency on its funds and policies (for details see Chapter V) is, among other things, responsible for the extensive usage of community terminology among members of the Matnas staff. To quote one of them, "American Jews know what community is all about. They wouldn't understand what a 'neighborhood' is, let alone a 'deprived' one. If we are interested in a constructive relationship with them, we ought to have some common language."

The other side of the coin is clearly the fact that in negotiations with the State's authorities in charge of the project, the concept was novel and, therefore, ill-defined and its value and importance undisputable. Thus, an initial parity in bargaining positions regarding terms of reference was created. This equal footing in communication facilitated official contacts by making the accepted ambiguity of "community" into a basis of interaction far removed, albeit temporarily, from the real imbalance of power between the two parties.

The fact that the great majority of Arod's residents remain unaware of or uninterested in those activities and projects cannot be overstated. In view of our discussion of the project's concern with publicity, the second option of being uninterested should be taken as a point of departure for the following.

Visible attendance of public functions is often a misleading yardstick for assessing the rate of participation. To begin with, in the case of Arod, it is repeatedly confirmed by project organizers that the same sector of the local population takes part in most events, while the rest remain indifferent and rarely show up.

While residents admit that they are kept reasonably well-informed about project activities and that their absence from such functions is not the fault of the organizers, they also state their lack of interest and motivation to partake in any public event. When asked to account for this attitude, many of them argue that they simply are not attracted by what is offered and that their daily routine is too full and excessively busy to accommodate such activities. Nevertheless, many insist that those activities that might benefit their children or provide inexpensive entertainment would be most welcome and desired. Encounters with residents reveal that most of them, although being well aware of the availability and even of the titles of activities, are nevertheless unfamiliar with the meanings and the expected content of those titles. Thus, projects that might have been chosen to suit the desires and the needs of a resident are discounted for lack of understanding of the label entitling it. Hence, abbreviated professional jargon, as well as cultural euphemisms, for example, "disengaged youth" for juvenile delinquents, made little sense, and rather than evoking interest mystified residents even further.

It is interesting to note that none of the residents regard the activities offered as stigmatic or offensive. Hence, neither the distinction between "welfare" and "community," nor the conception of the significance of the collectivity are impregnated into the tissue of the grass-roots construction of reality. The fact that most residents do not consider Arod as a social enclave, but rather as a residential neighborhood that is part of one's many worlds of existence, also furnishes that view.

Although residents do not look upon the project as a patronizing charity, and, therefore, are free of the web of feelings associated with the receipt of assistance, one cannot escape the impression that their passive reluctance to participate in its activities is imbued with a strong tint of alienation. However, this is not a result of a "cultural gap" or "social deprivation," but reflects their conviction that the main objective of Project Renewal is in the area of housing and material betterment. Thus, many residents do not see the relevance of the role of the social project in contributing toward this goal. The question of the origin and the consequence of the incongruity between the "community"-geared project and the residentially-oriented residents underpins the main line of discussion in the following section.

Having delineated the contours of Arod as a Project Renewal sponsored neighborhood, we proceed to a detailed ethnographic account of the impact of some of the problematics of the community-generating project on life in the neighborhood. Before embarking on this course of paradoxes, a few intermediary comments are necessary to interlink the general exposition hitherto depicted and the following discussion. This is done by way of offering a number of reflections on the main premises underlying the project. This is by no means an attempt to discount, discredit, criticize or reform certain aspects of the project. Rather, it is a set of viewpoints and conceptions held by project staff and elicited solely from field data. Although this material does not necessarily draw on the official ideologies adopted by the national project, it does derive a great deal of its phrases and metaphors from communications promulgated by its officials. Such utterances are made not as a reiteration of official policies, but as figures of speech employed to conceptualize and label certain convictions and positions regarding the operation of the project. In this sense, the fact of their presence in the field serves as a sufficiently cogent rationale for their inclusion in this discourse.

The undercurrent nature of some of those conceptions makes the task of uncovering the implicit meanings behind the overt everyday running of Project Renewal an extremely intricate decoding process. Nevertheless, as nebulous and unsubstantiated as such notions might seem, they are worthy of consideration and discussion as the socially determined cognitive parameters that guide Arod's version of the project. It should be stressed that it is precisely because of the unawareness of such fundamental ideas that they are rendered less manipulable than pronounced views and policies.

In contrast with extensively debated and continuously interpreted manifest values and practices of the project, the underlying principles that constitute its sociocultural foundation remain untouched and unaddressed. Yet, although elusive and obscure at times, those principles affect the project in a manner and extent deserving close examination.

The first premise on which the whole edifice of the project is constructed concerns the unquestionable desirability of a "community" life for the people in the neighborhood. Because a great deal of the meanings and problems embedded in this concept have already been examined (see Chapter I, section IV), we shall concentrate on those aspects of the idea of "community" that are not subject to public discussion. Such is, for example, the conviction shared by all members of project staff that the rudiments for community life are latently present in the existing patterns of relationships in the neighborhood; therefore, the main role of Project Renewal is to bring them into relief by exposing the residents to community projects and thereby extracting the potentialities in store.

Furthermore, this principal course of action is never called into question as one of many alternative approaches. The absolute desirability of community is set as the ultimate objective to be accomplished by the project. Thus, accompanied by a host of related ideas such as residents' participation and "positive self-image," the notion of a community has become an end to itself, a model of social life to be adopted and a paradigm for ideal identity to be pursued. The question of the relationships between residents' worlds and aspirations on the one hand, and the ideal presented to them in a form of "community," on the other, appears to escape the thoughts and plans of project workers. In fact, as indicated previously, that is the only way of treating the people as "cases," as if the "community" does not exist and inversely, of building a "community" as though the residents are not there.

The implications of such a stance are manifold because it enables the staff to belittle or to overlook altogether the whole context of socioeconomic components of life in Arod. So adamant is that viewpoint and so determined are staff members to uphold it, that the dual image of Arod resists any attempts of correction by introducing competing conceptions into discussions concerning the nature of the neighborhood.

Another feature of the concept of "community" concerns the occurrence of change and transformation. Being an ideal rather than a reality, the construction of "community" is static and unremittently immutable. This is not to say that the road to creation of "community" is not termed a dynamic and ongoing progress. There is a wealth of such terms and no effort is spared to emphasize that the project would be inconceivable without motives of mobility and advancement as its prime concerns.

This contradiction in terms of reference can be resolved if the two sets of images are considered within their respective different contexts. While the former—that of lack of change—is devised and developed to form a view of the residents that corresponds to their other attributes as helpless individuals, the latter serves to reinforce the vision of a community-creation process divorced from its incumbents. Evidently, such a dichotomy enables staff to pursue their declared goals and to engage in interests and power struggles regardless of the people, who are designated to the object of the whole operation.

Undoubtedly, a major contribution to the formation of such attitudes is the acute awareness among staff of the impending termination of the project. The breach between the idea of creating a viable community and the likelihood of attaining this within a reasonable and controllable span of time is caused by the conviction that the days of the project-sponsored community are numbered and long-term plans would be nothing short of a futile exercise.

Thus, implicit in running the project is also the assumption that the standard of living and quality of life are not imperatively connected to personal progress and individual careers. Because services and facilities are provided by the "community," and as individual existences are no reflection of the collective being, people in the neighborhood can expect a constant and steady improvement in their lives without the backing of socioeconomic status. Furthermore, personal plights and hardships can be excluded from the determinants of one's gains and benefits. Again, the equally distributed unearned endowments to "members of the community" do not seem to have any bearings on social life or social dynamics; it is an abstract idea rather than a viable reality.

To compliment these assumptions, staff members often advocate that there is a link between the development of "community" and the economic situation in the neighborhood, for a thriving community renders the area desirable. Consequently, property values will rise and residents will be encouraged to stay on and commit themselves to life in the neighborhood. Due to the physical projects, the first part of that hypothesis was proven right by the boom in prices of homes in the area. However, the second part was utterly unsubstantiated. The rise in the value of property only gave residents an extra inducement and confidence to look for alternative accommodations elsewhere. Residents rarely attributed this positive change to the impact of the community. On the contrary, a large number of them claimed that the increased desirability of the neighborhood as a residential area occurred despite the "cultural and the social standard" of its residents. The change was fully bestowed on the work of the physical project, which has turned Arod into a "clean, green and nondilapidated surrounding—a place that you don't have to be ashamed to live in"—to quote one of the residents.

The origin of the assumption that no matter what happens in the neighborhood residents will always stick to living in it, should be traced to another premise that dominates the preconceptions of the staff. This is the belief that the Arod neighborhood, and for that matter any neighborhood, is a closed system composed of a confined territory circumscribed by defined geographical boundaries and accommodating an impregnable social milieu. Outside forces such as the central government, the municipality and social and occupational ties are not considered to impinge upon that enclave. Rather, their impact is supposed to be sustained and regulated by the staff.

Apart from the added dimension to the image of a static community, this conception also conceives of the range of choices and opportunities open to residents as being restricted to life in the neighborhood. The world beyond the invisible boundaries of Arod seems to be irrelevant and even dangerous, because residents are not to be trusted in dealing with them. This exposure to external influences has to be carefully prepared, delicately handled and entirely controlled by the experience and knowledge of staff members.

These two dimensions of constructing the underlying cognitive foundation of the project—the unchanging and closed nature of "community"—made for the emergence of yet another component in that overall conception. This is the unspoken assumption that the basic coordinates of social life in the neighborhood always remain constant. Prediction for future changes are thus hinged on the tacit conviction that the course of "development and growth" in the neighborhood is a teleological unbending and irreversible path leading toward the anticipated end of "community."

Although awareness of demographic changes is voiced at times, it is regarded as more of a reason to precipitate the process of "community creation," which short of halting the inevitable change, would "resettle" and "redress" the upset balance. Since no accounting for how, who and when was offered, this recognition can only serve as yet another myth of the boundless potency of the idea of "community," the boundaries of which were neither human nor territorial.

NOTES

1. Although the Hebrew word *shechuna* lexically means both "neighborhood" and "borough," it is invariably employed, colloquially as well as officially, in the former sense. Furthermore, *shechuna* is a term usually reserved for deprived urban residential areas, although the media would often care to qualify if by adding the identifying noun-cum-adjective *oni*, meaning poverty/poor, or *metzuka*, meaning distress.

2. Netanya is a town of approximately 100,000 inhabitants situated between Tel Aviv and Haifa with an easy access from the main coastal road connecting the two cities. Its population is ethnically, economically and occupationally heterogeneous, although it should be noted that being a popular seaside resort, the town has a thriving tourist industry. Surrounded by agricultural settlements and kibbutzim, having a fairly big industrial area of its own, and being in such close proximity to Tel Aviv, employment opportunities are ample and there is no shortage of seasonal work.

3. Menachem Begin, the Israeli prime-minister at the time of the research, was the most revered public figure among residents. Enjoying almost unreserved respect, his name was frequently invoked in connection with the perceived good fortune of Israeli society in general, and Arod in particular.

4. The term "Ashkenazi," which literally means "German," refers to the Jews of Western (i.e., European and American) origin. They are contrasted with the "Spharadim" (literally, "Spanish"), the Jews of Spain, North Africa, and Arab countries.

5. It should be noted that unlike in some quarters of the Diaspora, where synagogue membership is taken to ensure Jewish burial arrangements, such matters are taken care of in Israel by the state. Hence, this factor must be ruled out as a reason for attending synagogue activities.

6. Although rooted in some religious connotation, the term *kehila*—community, in Hebrew, is mostly used in secular contexts. Being, like many other modern Hebrew locutions, an old term linguistically modified to suit new needs, it is infused with meanings strictly reserved to the world of civic matters. Moreover, it is worth noting that the word is by no means as extensively used in Hebrew as it is in English and thus, from a sociolinguistic point of view, it is a relatively unladen term amenable to contain newly introduced connotations. Hence, its suitability to serve as a viable linguistic tool in a nascent social situation, such as the case under discussion.

Chapter III

The Dilemma of
Cultural Identity:
Involvement Versus Stigma

The constitution of the social world of community does not happen in a symbolic vacuum. The array of characteristics implied by the status of Project Renewal neighborhood includes economic deprivation, ethnic labeling and political powerlessness. More important, those attributes in the context of Israeli culture invariably involve a whole gamut of stigmatic images ranging from educational backwardness through poor hygiene and violent behavior to present-oriented gratification and reliance on extended families and the state. The fact that Arod, multiethnic, economically strong and politically potent, possesses none of the corollaries of "cultural deprivation," does not prevent its residents from falling prey to that imagery. As individuals, residents rarely define themselves in ethnic or "welfare" terms, but as members of a newly-found community. The problem of reconciling their imputed collective cultural heritage and social background with the establishment of a past-free, stigma-cleansed and modernity-oriented entity becomes a predicament.

Furthermore, before the advent of a community-charged environment, encounters with stigmatic connotations were sparse and promptly dealt with on an interpersonal basis. Now that the neighborhood is being made a tool with which a new identity is to be forged, the social world of community flood-light the recesses

73

of cultural identification which were previously dimmed and almost forgotten.

The public rituals of becoming a community are thus inbued with images of other social worlds, and residents find themselves contending with yet unfamiliar but compelling dilemmas of being "ethnic" versus being "Israeli"; of being prone to violence and uncleanliness versus the imperatives of "clean and green" surroundings; and of being a disinterested inhabitant versus the expectation of total commitment as a resident.

The ambivalence of shrugging off stigmatic badges, on the one hand, and reinforcing them, on the other, is expressed in a variety of patterns of behavior, each of which counteracts the other. Thus, while involvement and participation are regarded as being conditioned by shunning away from stereotypes of ethnic origin, violence, unruliness and deprivation, the ways and means of achieving this restores the poignant sense of inferiority and reinstates the low self-image of residents.

I. NEUTRALIZING THE IMAGE OF DEPRIVATION

Stereotyping Arod as a violence-stricken area has been one of the most predominant characterizations of the neighborhood fostered by residents and staff alike, and often reinforced by outsiders. Yet, the sources of that indisputable "program" are usually isolated and confined to a defined category of people sharing two common denominators: they are mostly nonresidents and their behavior is attributed to a pathological condition, an incurable mental affliction that pushes them toward assuming an antisocial conduct. Neither circumstances nor sheer greed can account for vandalism, theft, mugging, robbery and murder. Violent crime is deemed rooted in an irredeemable predisposition for idleness coupled with inconsideration and callousness.

A show staged by the local entertainment group includes a sketch portraying a "poor Arod family." The mother is a weepy, caring, hard-working woman; the father is a chronic lay-about and one of their sons is an idle boy who persistently rejects reasonable and remunerative employment offers. Even when he takes up a job as a printer, he is too lazy to persevere, and despite desperate attempts by concerned residents, he quits. However, his brother, who lives under the same conditions is an industrious, keen student who works laboriously toward a better future for himself. Indeed, he succeeds and the fruit of his efforts is a highly acclaimed academic career. Alas, no hope or advise is offered to his sibling, who is doomed to a life of ill-repute.

The coordinator of sports activities in the Matnas prides himself in having good contact with the local youth. Enjoying much respect and trust, he is approached by some friends of a convicted criminal, an Arod resident, who has been put on probation following a suspended jail sentence. The sports coordinator, who has vouched for the man's good conduct, is not surprised when the man is found guilty of another offense and thus ends up in prison. What seems to be a betrayal of personal faith is interpreted by the coordinator as inevitable. He states his conviction that "once a criminal, always a criminal. He has got it in his blood."

According to Matnas staff, the rot is set in Arod by a few families with a history of criminal records. These "elements" are "lost cases" whose bad influence must be monitored, kept in check and, if necessary, eliminated. The rest of the population, however, is said to be law-abiding and whose notoriety was unjustly attributed. This assertion is often illustrated by examples of unexpectedly good behavior displayed by some of the residents best known for their vile tempers and disrespect for the law. The transformation in conduct is considered to be one of the most astounding achievements of the "community." Thus, many references are made to the fact that the glass doors of the temporary Matnas remain unsmashed, and the premises are still intact. The director even proposes to remove the protecting grids from the local billboards since "we are not any more in the precivilized bronze age. We are in the renewal era."

Behind the declarative assertion of Arod as a violence-free area is concealed another attitude that, although less pronounced, is impregnated in many actions and interactions. This is the view that not only is Arod riddled with crime and violence, but that "lack of proper values" is endemic to the neighborhood. The alleged "facade" of law and order in Arod is often assailed by quips and jokes indicating a trait of unrestrained aggression inherent in the residents. A proposed boxing match to be held as part of public entertainment is rejected sardonically because "the people here will expect real blood," and the organizers are subsequently advised not to initiate contests and competitions that might test the residents capacity to contain their violent proclivities.

Although members of staff pay ample lip service to means of reducing crime, such as reinforcing the civil guard patrols and calling on the police to allocate more police force for the neighborhood, they all share the conviction that as crime cannot be eradicated, it is essential to the image of Arod as a transformed area. Thus, regardless of police records that attest to the claim that the crime rate had dropped, members of staff hold on to their ambivalent view of Arod as both a crime-afflicted area and a peace-loving, order-seeking community. This is evidently another facet of the division between the idea of community and the "reality" of people.

This cognitive paradigm is further corroborated by applying it to some other aspects of the image of deprivation. Perhaps most noted is the attitude toward those residents in need of welfare services. Generally speaking, the project advocates an unequivocal separation between welfare and community. Thus, the elderly who are in need of support services such as supplementary benefits, home help and mental care are regarded as the "clients" of the social workers. However, those areas in the life of old people that symbolize "involvement" in communal activity are attended to by the Matnas in the form of an old-age club, trips for the elderly, and so forth. Personal needs and daily programs are excepted from the domain of the project and thereby, from the idea of Arod as a community. Pleas by residents to have a hearing by project staff are rejected on the grounds that the Matnas is not geared to handle personal plights, and thus the applicant would invariably be referred to the appropriate welfare agency.

II. CLEAN NEIGHBORHOOD—
"DIRTY" RESIDENTS

"Clearing up the community" from order-disturbing elements takes its most illustrative from in the concept of hygiene, cleanliness and their opposites—dirt, squalor and slovenliness. To quote one of the project workers, "Dirt is also a form of violence." Observing public order in shows and other community functions is often correlated to refraining from strewing litter and keeping the place tidy. The physical project is much lauded for giving Arod a new look of suburban green and white complexion. A top item in the list of the project long-term priorities is a massive operation of removing major rubbish dumps from the area and taking legal action against those residents who turn their backyards into a site for junk or any other "improper" use. As for short-term plans, the project, as well as the residents, are preoccupied nearly to the point of obsession with what they consider to be Arod's main insoluble problem—dirt.

The urgent need for stricter hygienic discipline in the neighborhood is an unanimously agreed upon subject, which, irrespective of the actual state of cleanliness in Arod, is regarded as the key to a "healthy" community life. Residents, seconded by members of staff, complain about the noncaring attitude of people in the neighborhood whose standards of personal hygiene and concern for the aesthetics of their surroundings are beneath contempt.

Thus the equation: hygiene = order = aesthetics = moral virtues = good community, is upheld by members of the Matnas staff as the ideal model for renewing Arod. Implicit in this model is the unspoken distinction between the neighborhood and its residents, a division that conceives of residents as dirty, disorderly and violent, and therefore neither capable of maintaining an aesthetic environment, nor deserving to live in one. Again, people are cast away from ideas and individual life is not supposed to impinge on the emergence of community life.

The impaired self-image, the awareness of that distinction and the association between the Matnas and such images of residents are perhaps best sketched out in a cartoon that appeared in an issue of the local newspaper, commissioned by the Matnas and edited by members of staff. It shows human cargo being unloaded from the back of a tipper lorry with one of the persons saying to another, as they were both rolled down to the ground, "I am fed up with the cheap trips of the Matnas." The range of images evoked is almost self-evident. The residents are likened to a rubbish heap and are handled in the same manner of impersonalized revulsion and disdain as the disposal of real rubbish would warrant. The Matnas, while discharging its duties to the community, treats the actual residents as nonentities, not even as raw material worthy of recycling and remolding. The residents are nothing short of a nuisance and an impediment to the successful operation of the project.

The question of the rudimentary causes for the unbridgeable gap between the ideal of accomplishing a community and the unaccomplished resident is rarely discussed openly. Nevertheless, meetings, encounters and public addresses are rife with clues and cues as to the origin of the incapacity of residents to live up to the required standards of communal participation. Such references, not unexpectedly, draw on the whole spectrum of ethnic prejudice and "in need of fostering" paternalism so deeply entrenched in many quarters of Israeli society.

However, due to the effects of the contradiction at hand, observable manifestations of such stances are scarce and not typical. Most of the expressions hinged around these motifs are inverted projections of stigmatic constituents, and as such reflected a complex picture of ambivalence and self-denying images. Thus, the ethnic dimension and its negation, coupled with the dilemma of assuming an Israeli identity within the boundaries of a "deprived" neighborhood, interplay to generate a collage of images that constitute the experience of being an Arod resident.

As described in Chapter II, the structure of social life in the neighborhood sets the scene for the various interpretations and competing meanings expounded by residents regarding their lives in Arod. The labile boundaries, the relatively reasonable housing conditions, the heterogeneous economic and ethnic structure and the constant demographic changes—all these factors and more make for a nonmonolithic fabric of behavioral patterns, symbols and lives. Thus, the creation of a "community" calls for monolithic devil's advocates, the most notable of which was the ethnic factor.[1]

III.   ETHNICITY RECONSTRUCTED

Two codes of handling ethnic matters governs the manner in which expressions of ethnic identity are shaped. The first is the emphasis on the multiethnic nature of the neighborhood, whereas the second gives a distinct priority to manifestations of ethnicity as a cultural origin while censoring any display of current ethnic folklore or worse still, popularized ethnic elements in everday life, and particularly in the world of entertainment.

The multiethnic characteristic of Arod is enunciated on a great number of public occasions and invariably in the same form, that is, as a parade of "authentic" ethnic symbols such as food, songs, dances, dramatization of customs, costumes, ornaments and domestic and religious handicraft and art. The festival of *Simchat Torah*, the rejoicing of the Law, as well as the *Mimuna*, the traditional Moroccan festival, and some especially designated events such as "an evening of ethnic groups" serve as arenas for root-searching, past-dwelling and ethnic-legacy boasting.

However, any spill-over to the field of popular folklore is strictly forbidden, and those public functions that do not withstand the scrutiny of being a "cultured, civilized" affair are not approved. Shows on the verge of what appear to the staff to be "vulgar," "unrepresentative' or "common" are unreservedly eliminated from the canonized repertory of local entertainment. Popular singers of oriental songs, whose reputation is gained through the circulation of music cassettes on a massive scale, rather than through the mass-media, are regarded by project staff as "good enough for family events, but not for the community." This distinction between families as units containing ethnic vestiges and the ethnic-free community draws on the previously discussed separation between residents and community. Thus, mockery of eastern accents, scorning ethnic-based bands and reviews using derogatory terms to describe the attendants of such performances are all part and parcel of the abuse of ethnic traditions as live and viable phenomena. However, self-declared ethnically-oriented per-formers who have gained nationwide recognition as representa-tives of modern Israeli culture are hailed as the ideal epitome of ethnic identity and, accordingly, their shows are booked and well-advertised.

Although ethnic divisions do not appear to affect relationships, and residents are not usually in the habit of identifying one another by ethnic stereotypes, ethnically-based self-denigration is a commonplace phenomenon. Like being violent and dirty, ethnic attributes seem in the eyes of the staff to be an innate existential quality of the residents. Hence, any attempt of destigmatization through the obliteration of ethnic insignia often generate a backfiring effect, reinforcing the undesirable image. Thus, when a proposed Moroccan sing-along show was found to be unsuitable due to its "vulgarity and the mockery it made of genuine Moroccan culture," a sneering suggestion was made to bring Shimon Peres to the neighborhood "to give them a bit of fun." (Peres, the leader of the Labour Alignment [the opposition at the time of the research], was known as a target for hatred and derision among Likud supporters of eastern origin.)

Attempts to appeal to ethnic divisions to recruit political support are few and feeble and, in any case, are met with unmitigated disapproval (see Chapter IV). However, because ethnic identity is firmly associated with religious affiliation, the ethnic factor is submerged into and absorbed by the religious one. As most residents described themselves as being, to a greater or lesser extent, "religious," and because the layout of local synagogues (see Chapter II) reflects the ethnic distribution in the neighborhood, the identification between the two seems to be fairly consistent. However, the reverence and respect addressed toward ethnically bound religious practices is not unreserved. When it comes to issues of relegating power within the project to religious-oriented staff and to mobilizing resources to declared religious functions, the director and most staff members are on their guard. Thus, a call for setting up a religious youth movement alongside the existing movement (see Chapter V) is rejected, and so are attempts to extend the range of religious classes and courses sponsored by the project. The latter is opposed on the grounds that the proposed teachers and instructors—mostly locally known Rabbis and other religious specialists—were unqualified to hold an officially recognized teaching position and, therefore, payments would not be approved by the project authorities.

This last point leads to the major predicament experienced by residents, that of earning an Israeli identity under the anathema of being ethnically, economically and socially stigmatized. Here the meaning of involvement in the neighborhood extends beyond the limits of Arod as a residential area and comprehends the self-image of residents as citizens of the state, and furthermore culturally legitimized full-fledged members of what they regard as "Israeli society."

IV. THE "ISRAELIZATION" OF AROD

The link transcending the deprived neighborhood into a visionary middle-class and suburban community is in those aspects of the project that introduce Arod to a taste of the "Israeli" experience of the affluent early 1980s. Indeed, Arod is impregnated with activities and symbols that are supposed to bring its residents, in spite of themselves, one step closer towards "the first Israel"—the opposite to the commonly used term "second Israeli," that is, the portion of the population originating in the mass immigration and the Maabarot inhabitants of the fifties. However, as with the previous issues, the attainment of "Israeli identity" is instilled in a process of foiling that very accomplishment, thus bolstering the barriers that represent the inability to achieve it in the past.

The regency of the Likud furnishes the idea that its constituency of electorate, that is, "second Israel," is no longer politically inferior, but at the same time fails to provide a set of symbols with which their supporters can identify. Instead, an alternative set of already available culturally established entities has to be sought. The system of surrogate images consists of nationalistic themes out of which the most appealing, and by far the most powerful, is the army.

Two factors help to establish the army as the core of Israeli identity in Arod. The first is the heterogeneity of the neighborhood, both socioeconomically and politically. Although project staff, as well as residents, carefully avoid any reference regarding their political sympathies, it is accepted that the political profile of the neighborhood is not monolithic. Although it is almost taken for granted that most of the residents pledge their allegiance to either the Likud or the National Religious Party, it is equally understood that to avoid conflict and controversy, the political issue must be shunned. On the few occasions that the subject was brought up, it was instantly hustled and dismissed as "irrelevant," "dangerous" or "dirty." The second factor is brought upon by force of circumstances—that was the war in Lebanon, which took place in the midst of the research, and whose impact on the life in the neighborhood had to be reckoned with.

The army as a unifying symbol of communal solidarity and unreserved loyalty to the state is invoked in most public events. Thus, on Simchat Torah, all the representatives of the ethnic groups composing Arod, while parading in front of the local crowd and the visiting delegation of the "sister community" from New Jersey, sent greetings and blessing to "our hero soldiers." The apex of the inauguration ceremony of the temporary Matnas was a donation made to *Leebee,* the foundation for the security of Israel. A similar donation was made by residents on behalf of Arod on a televised nationwide fund-raising event for the the same purpose. A military exhibition and a project-sponsored summer school modeled on a regimented martial hierarchy also became highlights of communal activity.

Enthusiastic and boundless as it is, the identification with military service as a symbol of nonethnic Israeli nationalism is, nevertheless, a problematic one. Arod is known as an area with a relatively low profile of recruitment due to exemptions and disqualifications on grounds of criminal record, family problems, drug usage and mental disturbances. This image has become nationwide with the production of a semidocumentary film based on the case of a conscript, an Arod resident, whose adjustment to army life turns out to be an obstacle course of desertion, disobedience and inability to adapt to disciplined orderly routine. Influenced by his eldest brother, whose criminal record is beyond redemption, intimidated by his friends and forced to help his widowed mother, the novice is torn between his ties and commitment to his past and his future aspiration to become a stigma-free law abiding citizen. Not surprisingly, the film was unpopular with Arod residents, who avoid any reference to it. Even in the wake of the broadcast of the film by the Israeli national television on the eve of Independence Day, the reaction was muted and somewhat indignant. As one resident stated, "This case doesn't represent us law-abiding peaceful Arod residents. It will only smear our name and damage the achievements of recent years."

The already tarnished image of Arod with regard to the army is one of the prime concerns of the project, which took great pride in the fact that Arod is the first neighborhood to initiate a special program for preparing delinquent and problematic youth for military service. Although there is little doubt as to the correctional values placed on this project by those who devised it, it is also clear that it contributes, to a large extent, towards reinforcing and furnishing the stigmas that are supposed to be erased by its operation.

Eradicating the "second Israel" from Arod by transforming it into a residential area modeled on the commonly held conception of a middle-class, up and coming suburbia, involves the adoption of a symbolic code intended to reproduce that kind of image. Because Arod lacks either the local heritage or the social networks to interweave its residents into what they conceive of as the fabric of Israeli culture, the symbols chosen as foci of identification are anchored in patterns of behaviors that seem to conform to a very broad common denominator prevailing in contemporary "first Israel" society.

Thus, computers, video games, a "country club" styled new Matnas and an English class for adults epitomizes the facet of modernity and progress in the image of the Israeli experience, while tours of the country, old-Yishuv (the pre-State organized Jews of Palestine) sing-alongs and folk dancing constitute the essence of some well-established insignia of the "first Israel." This mode of indiscriminate total identification with symbols remotely connected to the real world of Arod's residents reaches a point of absurdity in the following example: A composition written by a school child describes the elderly residents of Arod basking in the twilight sun, watching their golden-haired grandchildren—"the future of Arod." Significantly, the future generation of Arod is depicted in terms, even including the physical appearance, of the out-Arod world of Ashkenazi dominated suburbia.

The contrast between up-to-date facilities that play a part in the creation of "community" and the residents who are allegedly not ready to accept and absorb those means of producing such an entity, is demonstrated by yet another symbol of Israeli suburban life: the local newspaper. *Arodon,* the local newspaper of Arod, appears frequently although irregularly. Its editorial board consists of a few project workers who also contribute most of the reports and put in the announcements. The choice of material is supposed to give proper coverage to events and issues concerning the neighborhood. Thus, residents are expected to derive most of their knowledge about Arod's organized activities from the information provided by *Arodon.*

However, not only does *Arodon* present a picture of Arod abundant with problems and criticism, the residents are deemed not to receive the paper, or if they do, not to be able to read it. "Lack of awareness and interest" alongside "considerable illiteracy" are the main factors supposedly responsible for this state of affairs. On many occasions alternative means of conveying essential information have been suggested and implemented, such as leaflets written in foreign languages, a neighborhood crier using a megaphone, and so on. Here the role of the activists as circulating community information is crucial and, indeed, whenever such need arises, an immediate appeal is made to those defined as the local "activists" to give a helping hand.

V. ACTIVISTS: PARTICIPATION OF LIMITED LIABILITY

The task of disseminating Matnas information assigned to activists by project workers is indicative of the whole problematics of the residents' share in instituting the idea of "community." The ideology upheld by project staff regards the "activists" as both the spearhead for the construction of community and an indispensable link between the administration of the project and the "grass roots" of the neighborhood. However, the code of practice that is supposed to emerge from such conceptions does not follow the fundamental notion of participation and involvement advocated by the ideology. Not only is it geared to serve different functions, but it also hampers and sometimes averts and foils any attempt by residents to become part of the decision-making mechanism that determines the allocation of priorities and the subsequent distribution of resources of the project. Although the formal structure of the operation of the Matnas might suggest otherwise, the actual conduct associated with those entitled "activists" is of delimiting responsibility and curtailing potential power.

The term "activists," originally coined as part of the nomenclature of Project Renewal ideology, is used in Arod to denote those residents who take some active role in official local affairs or serve certain appointed functions in the activities organized by the Matnas. Such participation can range from involvement in a local election campaign, and attending committee meetings, to helping with the preparation of refreshments and safeguarding public order in project-held gatherings. Arod is one of many neighborhoods that has a special course run by the Matnas for "public activists" with the declared objective of training its students to become "community leaders."

The pool of recruits is drawn from two main sources. The first consists of Arod's veteran public figures whose past record of service on various committees, involvement in local power struggles and representation of certain interests, ethnic groups or residential areas within the neighborhood, has established them as the "traditional" leadership of the neighborhood. The second comprises young members of the Matnas, sometimes in their teens, organized and coordinated "community" groups such as the local youth movement (see Chapter V), instructors of social activities, both paid and unpaid, and occasional volunteers who are called to joining forces in times of need.

The outstanding differences in age, background, local status and functions are well reflected in the place in "community" affairs accorded to these two respective categories by the Matnas director. While the former are regarded as a potential threat to the operation of the project, the latter are given ample encouragement both in terms of allocation of assignments and tasks within the context of the Matnas, and in moral support in the form of participation in Matnas general staff meetings and wide publicity of their contribution to the successful accomplishment of "community" enterprises in local communication channels. The participants of the course for public activitists, meetings of which were closed and the material delivered a well-kept secret, are neither approached nor claimed to have a significant share in the distribution of responsibilities in the running of neighborhood affairs (for more details, see Chapter V).

The elder "activists" are often described by the Matnas staff as "a quarrelsome and cantankerous lot whose interest in the public good is restricted to their own self-glorification." Somewhat muted criticism of the old leadership is also voiced by residents who maintain that as those well-known figures are not associated with the noted improvements in the physical face of the neighborhood, they must not claim credit for introducing them. This line of argument is reinforced and to a certain extent takes the form of a vicious circle, by the malfunctioning of the project's joint committees of staff and residents. Those community organs are irregularly convened and grounded to a halt by the absence of elected representatives due to procrastination tactics employed by several interested persons in the neighborhood (see Chapter IV).

In discussions held in Matnas meetings, the subject of residents' participation in running the project is often broached by the community worker (see Chapter V) as a point of criticism leveled against the director, who is accused of hampering grass-root direct involvement in decision-making processes. A twofold counter argument is usually used to refute such an allegation. Residents are referred to as both incapable of deciding what is good for them and incompetent to cast a professional judgment, let alone carry out executive duties, concerning the administration of the project. Thus, the steering committee is nicknamed "the chatter-box committee" and the "activists" attending its sessions "pseudo-leaders and mock representatives." The case for restricted involvement is often made on the grounds that a number of project staff members, first and foremost the director himself, are Arod's residents and thus satisfied the need for residents' representation. The fact that such a claim defeats the previous claim of "objective professionalism" as a prerequisite for efficient management, although it did not escape the attention of staff, seems to pose only a trifle inconsistency.

Nevertheless, following the local election, the overt attitude of project staff toward activists, at least those who were duly elected as representatives to the Arod committee, changed tone. Although most of the representatives were not new faces in the local arena, their status as impeccably elected residents credited them with a clean new public record, as yet untarnished. Hence, talk of cooperation, collaboration, "opening a new page," and "making a new start" was the order of the day. However, it took only a few weeks for the euphoric atmosphere to be recharged with previous tensions and conflicts. The newly elected representatives were accused of "apathy" and "selfishness," and project staff of "untrustworthiness" and "inconsideration."

With allegedly politically incompetent veteran leadership, on the one hand, and a generation of keen, but inexperienced youngsters incapable of taking over, on the other hand, the position of a "community" broker assigned to "activists" is bound to remain unfulfilled. Therefore, the duties earmarked for the available "activists" by project staff are all in accordance with the assumption that the residents' ultimate accomplishment of a "community" lifestyle is to observe the set of rules of conduct that would not demonstrate their stigmatic attributes. Thus "activists" became project appointed guardians against neighborhood anticommunity pitfalls, a position that is accurately mirrored by the range of functions performed by the "activists."

Acting as stewards in marshalling order in public gatherings and events organized by the Matnas is the most frequent task that "activists" are asked to perform. This is normally coupled with preparing the designated premises, keeping an eye on the behavior of the audience during the event and cleaning up the place afterward. Arrangements for such occasions are made meticulously well in advance and there is constant trepidation that the "activists" might not turn up on time or, alternatively, would default in discharging their duties. This mistrust, which incidentally is rarely founded, is shared by both staff and "activists" and met with no challenge from either. Having no official authority to impose discipline or to restore disturbed order, the presence of the "activists" on such occasions is more of a symbolic endorsement of staff members who have "to resort to using them" as one member put it and another added, "Often they are all we have to got in the community."

Another focus of stigma-handling by "activists" is the operation of house committees of apartment blocks in the neighborhood. Those are considered to be the most genuine representatives of grass-root residents' involvement, and as such occupy a revered place in all formal presentations of the project. This is the only category of residents that is allocated a budget and some office space in the Matnas—neither of which is nearly fully utilized. Notwithstanding the significance of that fact, the assigned functions of those committees are directly related to the image of one of the most predominant aspects of Arod as a "deprived area." Cleanliness, tidiness, sanitation, book-keeping and gardening are the tasks expected to be performed by such committees. Evidently, similar roles are assumed by most house committees of apartment blocks in Israel. However, only in Project Renewal-administered neighborhoods are such committees organized, instructed and monitored under the governing assumption that their performance requires supervision and guidance of a better informed, more "progressive" community-oriented body. In turn, the product of this educational process is intended to be imparted to the rest of the residents.

This intermediatory role follows a pattern with some other project-induced tasks assigned to "activists" to cover more stigma-imbued areas. Resident students are called upon, without much success, to provide tutoring to backward school pupils. Mothers who attend "good motherhood" courses are recruited to instruct other mothers, and members of the local youth movement are asked to guide their parents and peers in keeping Arod a tidy and well-mannered neighborhood. In short, stigma reinforced by involvement and vice versa creates the vicious circle of the second dilemma of the social world of community in Arod.

NOTE

1. Not surprisingly, the issue of ethnicity has preoccupied socioanthropological research in Israel for decades. For some references to relevant trends, see Weingrod (1979).

Chapter IV

The Political Dilemma:
Autonomy Versus
Intervention

Community creation in terms of cultural underpinnings is merely the framework for the pursuit of interests, the allocation of resources and the advancement of careers in the name of community.[1] This is also the arena where residents and staff alike are entangled in a battle to define areas of influence and to shape the power structure of the neighborhood. Thus, the complex tangle of views, conceptions and images discussed in the previous chapter comes into being and manifests itself through sets of interactions and situations embedded in the everyday running of the project. Values, symbols, attitudes and orientations, alongside meanings and contradictions, would be an unintelligible nonsense without the observable reality of social relationships from which they emerge, and without which addressing them would remain merely a scholastic exercise. Hence, the current chapter takes up the almost impossible challenge of examining and explicating the myriad of factors entailed in the daily operation of the project, thus offering a more tangible basis for the material presented in both the previous chapter and the ensuing one.

Intricate and multifaceted as it is, the administration of the project lends itself to analysis in terms of the second paradox—that of the striving for autonomous, free of outside tampering, community organization and operation versus the increasing need to preserve such autonomy by means of admitting a considerable extent of intervention (see Shimshoni 1983 for a broader perspective on Project Renewal intervention policies). Evidently, the whole rationale for this contradiction derives from the assumption made by those involved in the project that Arod is a social enclosure. Otherwise, because the neighborhood and its socioeconomic surroundings are indivisible (see Chapter II), such interpretation would prove to be a misguided tool for understanding.

Indeed, the problem of delineating the external boundaries of Arod stands at the heart of the dilemma of self-sufficiency versus dependency, and a critical analysis of the material at hand will show that it is handled and regulated in a manner corresponding to the factors involved in marking locally perceived definitions of the relation between "in" and "out." It will be argued that a great deal of the procedures implemented in the day-to-day operation of the project activities are governed by two strong organizing principles of shaping relationships. Together they generate a mode of behavior that, while constituting sharp distinctions between conceptions of Arod and images of the outside world, blurs, dims and smooths out differences and divisions within the neighborhood. This phenomenon by no means indicates lack of conflict and absence of discord. On the contrary, by rendering interests, goals and definitions ambiguous and equivocal, the potential arena for "misunderstandings," opposition and claims of all kinds become wide open. By the same token, it will be useful to note the ample ground for cooperation and flexibility that such a state of affairs provides for the participants.

Notwithstanding the significance of that aspect, the consistency of such a pattern is essential for sustaining the argument that an accepted nebulous conception of the field of action by its participants and a set of clearly marked borders surrounding it, enables the facade of a self-contained independent local entity, meaning, the "community," to thrive even in the face of growing dependency on the "outside." Only ambiguity and fuzziness can permit the maintenance of encounters and interactions as though they occur in a social vacuum and at the same time, by not exposing or suggesting external influence, allow intervention to affect the context of relationships. The range of tactics and stratagems employed to engender obscure definitions of situations and thereby set the scene for the preservation of dependent autonomy will be the subject of the following.

I. CLERKS AND CLIENTS

The project as a center for the allocation and distribution of services posed a twofold problem for members of staff vis-à-vis the recipients of that assistance. The first concerns the nature of the relationship between supposed "community" developers acting within and for the neighborhood and residents who are thought to become the incumbents of that "community." The brinkmanship of avoiding the risk of being seen by residents as patronizing do-gooders, and at the same time mustering enough authority to be able to act as efficient and trustworthy administrators, characterize much of the maneuvering displayed by the staff in the course of interaction with residents. The second facet of this relationship is the self-defeating treatment of residents as welfare cases, for such cases are contrary to the very idea of "community," and require resources that are unconstructive and therefore wasteful on the part of the "community" oriented worker.

Ideologically, the problem is resolved by applying concepts of sharing, equality and immersion and involvement to the relationship between staff and residents and to the status of members of staff within the neighborhood. Thus, the fact that the Matnas employed a large number of residents is extensively used to obliterate any conceivable distinction between externally imposed officials and the local population. Because the positions occupied by Matnas resident-workers are right across the board of hierarchy and role structure, no allegation of discrimination and prejudice are made. Instead it is regarded as a testimony for the Matnas being a "community center" in the true sense of the term. The open-door policy, no admission charge to most functions, the presence of "activists," and an overall informal approach to contact with residents—all are viewed as attesting to lack of officialdom and to an insignificant distance between project staff and "grass-roots" residents. In fact, a strong opposition is often voiced to the use of the terms "we" versus "they" with regard to the distinction between the two categories.

In practice, however, the picture is quite different, for the organization of Matnas functions is governed by interests, conflicts and conceptions rather irrelevant to the above description. The social workers, whose main interest is with welfare cases and "problem areas" within the neighborhood, pose a threat to the Matnas' commitment to the idea of a trouble-free community. Handling the fringes of the neighborhood is not just a drain on resources that could be better utilized elsewhere, but a re-endorsement of the stigma-fraught "anticommunity" elements in Arod. Because the elimination of such constituents, desirable as it might be, is nevertheless impossible; the only solution at hand is to erect an insuperable barrier between welfare and community.

This separation takes the form of lack of feedback information between the team of social workers and the social organizers. Avoidance, clashes and a wide use of professional jargon to muffle intentions and to block communication are commonplace in the interactions between the two. Although both parties act under the umbrella of the project, the former clearly identify themselves with governmental and municipal authorities to whom they are accountable, whereas the latter view their employment with the Matnas as the hub of their occupation.

It should be noted that the turnover among Matnas staff is relatively high, and most employees engaged by the project treat it as a transition post along their career path. This is partly due to the uncertainty with which many workers conceive of the whole of Project Renewal, and partly to the nature of employment offered by the Matnas which, in many instances, does not require specific qualifications or training. The social workers however, who are attached to a set career line with the security, incentives and commitment entailed by it, view the project as a passing assignment controlled by pseudo-professionals and aiming at the wrong targets. Indeed, these fundamental differences are expressed in the same jargon of "community," only the meanings imparted to it are worlds apart (see Chapter V).

This division manifests itself in allotting two separate premises to the two teams. The social workers, still under the sign and the title of Project Renewal, use a flat in the heart of Arod's most impoverished area, whereas the project headquarters moved to the temporary Matnas near Arod A. Due to a shortage of space and, perhaps for several other reasons, the operation of the Matnas is scattered around the neighborhood and the nature of the relocation is also with reason.

The main office, including the administration and the meeting room, are housed in one building with the director and the sports coordinator—the two contestants for power—permanently working there. The second echelon of staff, that is, the youth organizer, the youth movement coordinator and the cultural activities coordinator, are placed in an old but renovated community center. The rest of the workers make use of six public air-raid shelters and one flat in the neighborhood.

The dispersed activities impose a restraint on coordination and cooperation among staff members, who derive most of the knowledge concerning their colleagues' engagements from the weekly staff meetings held at the head office. Those meetings do not include the social workers, who consequently lose track of the Matnas operation. A fact that should be mentioned in this context concerns the information unit containing a pool of comprehensive data on Arod. This unit was initiated, organized, run and controlled by the community worker whose office, as well as the unit, are situated in the premises allocated for the social workers. Although officially accessible to all members of staff, the unit is at the sole disposal of that worker whose interests and allegiances are dissident to those of the Matnas (see Chapter V).

Thus, the divisiveness among workers and their differentiated appeal to and concern for various sectors of residents make the quest for "community" and "participation" into a plea of no practical consequence. For their part, the residents find the layout of the project functions confusing and incomprehensible. Although most of them are apparently familiar with the location of the head office, they are unacquainted with the other sites and seem quite bewildered to find out about the decentralized Matnas. Only a few are aware of the distinction between the welfare unit and the rest of the project operation, and as the majority of residents visiting the Matnas premises make inquiries on matters of welfare, the perplexity had become even greater. Furthermore, because members of staff are known to residents by their first names rather than by their official roles, it is an arduous and complicated mission to locate and to approach them at the appropriate time and place. Thus, even when such a search is successfully accomplished, it ends up in a frustrating gesture of cordial fobbing off, advising them of a more opportune occasion for the next meeting.

II. POWER WITHOUT A BASE

The situation of the dispersed Matnas staff is one of the factors involved in constructing the project as an arena where conflicts are arrested before eruption, and disputes peter out into minor discords. Other factors are the high turnover of staff, the lack of specific professional qualifications required for employment by the project and the great number of part-time positions offered by it.

All these factors are part and parcel of the fundamental realization shared by all Matnas workers that the national project and its Arod branch are short-lived enterprises offering no future prospects in terms of career opportunities and accumulation of power. Furthermore, it has been the conviction of many of them that the more successful the Arod project was, the less inclined the authorities would be to continue it. The commonly accepted understanding that the days of the project were numbered forces most of the members of staff to foster an outward view towards alternative employment with the project being either a transitional spring-board or a temporary respite. Thus, the relative absence of power struggles within the project team results not only from structural factors, as suggested in the previous section, but reflects a considerable degree of uninterest and lack of incentive to pursue such struggles. Indeed, most of the interactions among members of staff should be viewed and explained in the light of the conceived terminality of the project.

Although the unearthing of personal ambitions is far beyond the scope and the purpose of discussion, their projection onto the project makes them manifest as well as relevant to its understanding in more than one way. First, carefully planned career prospects elsewhere impinge on the conduct of the worker not only in terms of attitudes and behaviors, but mainly with regard to externally drawn resources and attention. Thus, the notion of autonomy is backlashed yet again by the solicited intervention from the outside.

The director of the Matnas, whose professional aspiration looms beyond the local project, spares no effort to introduce a spirit of a business-like organization into the project. He demands immaculate exactitude in submitting reports, the preparation of Matnas operations and their timing. He maintains that the value of "orchestration" of activities and the precise execution of assignments cannot be overrated. Notions of controlled relations between input and output and the advocation of meticulous planning and rational thinking are regarded by him as the order of the day, not only as a means of eradicating the stigma of deprivation and backwardness, but also as ways of expediating communication with the authorities in charge of the project.

This last point is frequently manifested in the unbending adherence to the rules and regulations of the various bodies involved in the project. This is done in a overt and expressive manner, which left no room for any mistake regarding the image the Matnas endeavored to project. Guests and visitors are most welcome to inspect the premises, to attend meetings and to offer advice, and so are any interested organizations and other local projects. The idea of the Arod project setting an example for the rest of the country is very much entertained by the director.

Such an outlook might seem somewhat enigmatic in view of the prospective termination of the project. However, the fact that the operation of the Matnas is presented as a showpiece of efficient managerial performance might offer some insight into the ulterior motive behind this front.

Although no disagreement is voiced against that approach, there are attempts by other members of staff to divert the emphasis toward their own spheres of personal interest. The sports coordinator, whose main concern is in establishing and sustaining a power base among residents with the intention of becoming a "grass-roots" leader, insists on intensifying the appeal of the Matnas residents through offering more employment opportunities and enhancing outdoor activities. His ideas take shape in the form of participating in national sports competitions and contests, activities that won Arod a number of awards and trophies, and of police and army involvement in neighborhood public events. In either instance, like in the case of the director's approach, the concept of the autonomy of the project draws heavily on recognition and acceptance by the outside. In fact, both men base their power of persuasion on implied external resources, which each of them claim to have mastered.

Resorting to external resources to influence the running of the Matnas, while maintaining the image of self-sufficiency, requires a delicately balanced approach to the question of contacts and connections with the outside. The tactic often used in dealing with this problem is of obscuring information through noncommittal, ambiguous messages. This mode of communication is applied to a variety of issues and ranges from reducing contacts to a personal level of relationship to transcending the outside to an unreachable sphere of power. Thus, when a problem of obtaining a building permit from the municipality is raised, the director dismisses it altogether because, "the mayor is a friend of mine." At the same time anticipated budget cuts and the image of the Arod project in high places are treated as being beyond the limits of influence of staff.

Hovering between these two extremes of ultimate manipulability versus absolute unattainability are the widely discussed concepts of "the community" and "the residents." These amorphous entities are used in the service of any set of interests and are invoked to testify opinion or motions on the agenda. Being accountable to "the residents" or "doing what is best for the community" are frequently uttered phrases that charter almost any argument, claim or proposal made in the name of those elusive images. Wrangles erupt when evidence is produced to attest to an alleged "betrayal," "disregard," "nepotism" or "discrimination" or residents—all inexcusable offenses, which every member of staff is accused of committing at one time or another and all considered as "stabbing the community in the back," to quote one such accusation.

However loose and liberal usages of the terms "residents" and "the community" are, there are three distinguishable strains of views serving as main cores for debate and argument. The first, which is held by the director and most of the externally hired members of staff, advocates that "although we are working for the residents, we know best what is good for them." This claim for superior knowledge is made on the grounds that "we are also residents, but unlike the rest of them, we are professionals." A diametrically opposed view is voiced, usually in a very forceful manner, by the sports coordinator, who argues that "the Matnas is the residents and therefore should be run by them in accordance with their needs and expectations." He blames the rest of the staff for barring residents from full participation and using the project as a bandwagon on the road to their private careers. The third opinion, whose main exponent is the "community worker," takes a more legalistic stand on the matter and maintains that it is the duty and the jurisdiction of the Matnas to make the necessary provisions for adequate and satisfactory residents' representation in the Matnas. A fourth party of Matnas staff, consisting of residents with responsibilities for catering, maintaining and grass-roots organizing, never expresses its view nor does it take any position, not even by way of tacit implication. (For a discussion of the concept behind those stances see Chapter V.)

Because there is no way of settling such differences, and as those divisions merely reflected some fundamental conflicts of power and interest among staff, an agreed code of smoothing over, glossing and "brushing under the carpet" disputable issues is developed. It consists of phrases, platitudes, aphorisms and out-of-context jargon to label and mark all subjects vulnerable to contention and rift. This technique enables members of staff to avoid exposing themselves and their resources to the scrutiny of their colleagues, and at the same time to avoid risking a breakdown in the flow of interaction.

A representative selection of this terminology comprises phrases such as "assuming personal responsibility," "personal sacrifice and investment of our whole being in the community," "activism and dynamics," "vision, imagination and power of innovation," "revitalization and the development of a new tradition with every-thing we do," and so on. Although investment and resources are described as boundless, conditioned and restricted only by the extent of personal commitment to the project, the allocation of assignments and the measures taken to avert encroachment and duplication are steps in seemingly opposite directions. However, the function of this apparent contradiction is not to constitute a congruent worldview among members of staff, but to resolve a dilemma stemming from the nature of the project as a setting for the interplay of conflicting interpretations, obscure resources and unfounded claims for power.

As the operative aspect of running the project is separated from the discussion and arguments concerning meanings, objectives and rationales associated with it, members of staff develop a practical basis for working relationships. This is not done simply by eradicating the need for making sense of the work and the context, but by offering a broad, almost unlimited, ground for personal interpretation acceptable within the framework of a vague, but nevertheless binding, definition of long-term goals. As the realization that the project is about to be terminated soon overrides any other conviction or view, members of staff can conveniently comply with that set of unearthly impractical values. This, while presenting the investment in the project in terms of a non-zero sum game situation. The organization of the staff and the division of labor among them is carefully watched and explained as a zero-sum pool of resources contingent upon inexorable forces, such as the decisions of the national project and government policies.

The might and law imputed to authority not only inspires deference, but also serves a dual purpose. It provides an acceptable excuse on which to pin any lack of initiative or unwillingness to enter into negotiation with external agencies, thereby increasing the dependency of the local project on its benefactors, both in Israel and abroad. The second function is realizing that the Matnas is in no position to bargain for better terms with its resources to justify and implement other "nonconventional" methods in dealing with the authorities. The impression is generated that influence and persuasion can be only achieved through personal contacts, nonofficials, almost secret meetings, and the manipulation of situations and people to the advantage of the Matnas. Such clandestine operations are never revealed or even discussed, but members of staff can make a point of intimating such information, which invariably remains shrouded with mystery. Fragmented facts and equivocal messages are forever disseminated to create jigsaw puzzles with neither contours nor pattern to be pieced together. Indeed, on very few occasions did members of staff show sufficient motivation to solve them.

Thus, visits to the sister community, a meeting with a "top knob" in Jerusalem, a confidential document, or hearsay information concerning decisions affecting the project, are all used to furnish images of power and influence associated with the outside. This conceived impervious barrier is based on the highly centralized image of the project and on the realization that the core of the decision-making mechanism at government and Jewish Agency levels is impregnable to ideas and actions of local projects. This is interwoven into another conception of the relationships between those bodies. Staff members believe that due to lack of coordination and conflicting sets of interests, there are many loopholes and lacunas in the processes determining the fate of the national project. Hence the conviction that with wisely devised planning and shrewd maneuvering, such as the previously described tactics, hiatuses can be, and indeed should be, taken advantage of.

III. LOCAL LEADERSHIP— THE GUIDED AND THE MISGUIDED

With elusive power bases, precarious resources and an uncertain future, the staff of the project had to encounter the devious problem of forming attitudes regarding the emergence of neighborhood leadership. The dilemma was how to stand by the propagated notions of local autonomy and residents' participation without imperiling their own positions. Far from being unanimous on the interpretation of interests and objectives, let alone on matters pertaining to the role of residents in the project, all members of staff nevertheless display a joint disapproval of the preelection neighborhood leadership. This dissatisfaction stemmed from the commonly shared realization of those in Arod who occupy positions of leadership in official organs of residents' representation never duly elected, nor did they enjoy a widespread recognition as "community" stalwarts.

It was common knowledge that the members of the defunct neighborhood committee defend the interests of their own kith and kin and localized networks of supporters, and thus it was maintained by both residents and staff that those nonelected members were not to be entrusted with authority and responsibility concerning Arod's affairs. Even those members of staff who were at odds with the director acquiesced in the generally accepted view of the illegitimacy, inadequacy and inefficiency of the committee. This made discussions of residents' participation somewhat academic, because, all parties advocated the need of holding an election enshrined in the law, supervised by legal authorities outside the neighborhood, and thus providing a judiciously recognized basis for residents' involvement in the project.

Indeed, involvement in the project was considered to be the issue at stake for all members of staff, but for entirely different reasons. While the sports coordinator and his supporters were convinced that they would greatly benefit from the active participation of residents in decision-making processes, as they regarded themselves as unofficially acknowledged residents' representatives, the director and most of the other members of staff aim to install legally acceptable residents' representation in compliance with the required and expected profile of the project. Aware as they were of the significance of averting criticism on account of deficient residents' participation, most of their efforts were centered around being circumspect of any diversion of the prospective new committee from the function set for it as a mere token for grass-roots incorporation into the project.

Great pains were taken to ensure the legality of the election process and to involve as many independent outside officials as possible to supervise it. Long delays and procrastinations in the preparation of election day were explained as inadvertent consequences of the will to stick to the regulations and to avoid accusation of favoritism, nepotism and misconduct. Although some contestants regard the lengthy period of preparation as a delay tactic devised by the organizers of the election to prolong their unchallenged domination of the project, it was generally assumed that, as one of the "activists" stated, "A few months here or there will not make any difference; the people of Arod never change anyway."

Heightened awareness of external recognition stood in sharp contrast to the lack of interest in and inducement to internal processes. There was ample information circulated in the neighborhood concerning procedures of voting, location of ballot boxes and nomination of supervisory election committees. However, campaigning in the form of public gatherings addressed by candidates or distribution of candidates' platforms were nearly absent. Various explanations were offered to this phenomenon, all attesting to the conception of Arod's residents as being unprepared to assume civil responsibilities and to determine their own fate in a democratic fashion. Apathy and indifference were the primary interpretation with "illiteracy," "traditionally undemocratic background," "familial loyalties," and "lack of awareness of public affairs" as its specified components. The Matnas gave neither encouragement nor material support to sponsor the election on the grounds that such involvement might implicate the project in a political smear campaign. This although, overtly at least, the Israeli political arena had no bearings on the views expressed by candidates.

Such views took either the extreme form of vague, commonly held ideas of the public good toward which the candidate should aspire, on the one hand, or very specific demands concerning narrowly focused interests on the other. Thus, between slogans such as: "renewing the face of Arod," "residents for the community and the community for residents," "giving the residents a chance to express their true wishes," and so on, and the urgent need to repair a local sewer system or to build another ethnically centered synagogue, there was no intermediary level of concrete proposals based on a defined stance or formulated objectives. This attitude concurred with the observation that although most candidates paid some lip service to the idea of Arod as a united neighborhood and a cohesive community, there was very little in their suggestions and assertions to attest to this.

The fear of "misguided interests," that is, localized demands, interfering with the project's feat of "community" creation, governed many of the conflicts between members of staff, the most poignant of which was the disagreement over the eligibility of the sports coordinator to take part in the election as a candidate. Being confident of widespread popular support among residents, and being threatened with dismissal from the Matnas by its director, the sports coordinator decided to make a bid for local leadership. He cherished the hope that such a political gain would not only consolidate and safeguard his position within the Matnas, but would also serve as a springboard for controlling the project. Because he insisted that his involvement with the project, as opposed to that of his opponent, was based on a permanent interest in Arod's affairs that prelived and, indeed, would outlive the project, his claim for power was not contingent on the existence of the Matnas as a "community center." Indeed, he was the least committed member of staff to the use of the "community" terminology because for him, "Arod is where I live—a neighborhood." It is worth nothing that in the eyes of his opponents, the reluctance to adopt community jargon was an indication of a "narrow view of the neighborhood and inability to articulate ideas concerning the common good." In other words, for all cultural, stigma-laden purposes, he was treated as a resident.

A ruling issued by the judge in charge of the election forbade the sports coordinator's participation in the campaign and thus, in effect, reinforced the separation between the project and the direct involvement with the "grass-roots." This external intervention in widening the cleavage between the Matnas and the residents was yet another instance of the phenomenon of divorcing "community" from the people for whose benefit it is claimed to be intended. The action enabled the project to maintain the image of self-sufficiency and self-rule by residents while in effect it neutralized the potential power held by residents to operate efficiently through the Matnas. The latter would have become, in turn, an arena for local politics.

With 25 percent participation of franchised residents in a rainy working-day election, the labels of apathy and "cultural unreadiness" were instantly removed. The project prided itself on having yet another feather in its cap, a result of arduous work of cultivating the people towards taking up their roles as responsible residents. Although many representatives were reelected and the new committee was half-way close to being a replicated version of the old one, there was an initital reaction of unanimous approval and expressed delight with the results.

Belated responses, however, constituted a different attitude. The project director and his followers entertained the idea of "cooperating with the new committee," which would take the form of conferring some of them with positions of prestige and honor that would prove no hindrance to the control of the project. Such "ritualistic" roles were designed to satisfy the need for publicly recognized status attributed to the members of the committee and at the same time, provided a "community" figure of acknowledged stature with whom the residents could identify. This scheme was aborted by the sudden illness of the prospective chairman of the new committee and voices from within it in support of a more active mode of involvement and power sharing. These pleas soon became the cause of internal rifts and struggles among residents, which paralyzed the operation of the committee yet again.

The old-new local political stalemate, which was to the obvious advantage of the project's director, became a subject for applying "community"-oriented explanations and remedies. The conflicts were blamed on personally entrenched narrow interests and lack of "neighborhood awareness." No talk or discussions were spared to express discontent and to propose ways and means of "correcting" and guiding residents and particularly residents' representatives to adopt a more "positive" approach to the "community," and to recognize the power and the sense of fulfillment infused by such realization.

Demerited to serve the public, the members of the new committee were caught up in a resumed vicious circle of stigmatization entailing disqualifications engendering further labeling. Being under this constraint, they posed no serious threat to the Matnas. However, unlike the bridled committee, challenges of power were thwarted from other directions.

Sporadic spates of opposition to the leadership of the Matnas were launched from time to time either from inside, that is, by its own employees, or from outside, mainly by young residents, mostly students, who were critical of the way the project was run. Being conversant with the media, opponents used local papers of Netanya, and through correspondence and reporters aired their unsavoury views. Swift and decisive reaction of similar nature came in retaliation from the director, and the residents in question found themselves neutralized, divested of both their local power bases and of their Matnas employment.

Most of them ceased operating within the neighborhood and let their criticism lay dormant; a few found alternative employment elsewhere and even moved out of Arod with dwindling interest in its affairs. Again, the fact that the boundaries of the neighborhood were conceived of as selectively permeable contributed toward the ability of the Matnas to keep a check on mobilization of resources and the filtering out of undesired elements. Thus, constant definition and redefinition of boundaries is the subject of the following.

IV.   "IN" AND "OUT"— COMMUNITY AS COMMODITY

The manufacturing of "community" requires setting up signs to indicate directions in and out of the confines of that socially constructed enclave. Such pointers are not merely the product of prevailing images and concepts of "community," but serve a significant function in mobilizing resources in and out of the domain of the neighborhood. Because that domain is presented in terms of "community," so is the main bulk of activities, services and artifacts that constitute the framework of the project's operation. Thus, community as a defined entity can be negotiated, exchanged, dissolved and regenerated both internally and externally. In other words, elements of Arod's reality molded and labeled as part of "community" life are amenable presentation as commodities to be traded off with the outside world.

The two-way communication between Arod and its social surroundings as regulated by the project is governed by three organizing principles. First, certain elements of the perceived outside world are manifestly inducted and admitted into the neighborhood in exchange for tantamount returns. Second, approved components of "community" life are exported to the outside world in order to attain recognition and a reinforced sense of self-sufficiency. Third, those constituents within the neighborhood that did not seem to belong either to residents or to the conception of community are isolated and neutralized. A great deal of references concerning the application of this set of criteria in constructing the reality of "community" have already been discussed throughout this work, particularly in the previous chapter (see The "Israelization" of Arod, Chapter III, section IV). The purpose of the current analysis is to suggest a correlation interconnecting locally constructed concepts of community, boundaries and self-sufficiency. It is hoped that such a linkage will shed some light on the dynamics of relationships and actions embedded in the formation of a "community."

Admission of extra-neighborhood elements into Arod is regarded by members of staff as strictly conditioned by their relevance to the "community," that is, by the extent to which their presence can be exploited in the service of the project's interests under the guise of "a contribution toward the community." This ranges from using a national incident, such as political murder, to give a moral lesson on the detriments of violence, to the encouragement given to outside volunteers who organize local activities. Particularly welcome are officials representing government ministries, the Jewish Agency, municipal authorities and guests from abroad or from other Project Renewal areas. All of them are shown around, introduced to activists and expected to appreciate the accomplishments of the "community." Undoubtedly, such impressions are assumed to be either personally bandied or officially conveyed to the appropriate foci of decision making. Whenever such a visit is due, the whole organization of activities is expediently geared to provide the best possible presentation.

Hosting a guest within the confines of the Matnas and in the company of its staff is normally so well coordinated so as not to cause any embarrassment or disservice to the project. However, dignitaries, who in the course of their excursion into the neighborhood have to encounter the local population, are exposed to a somewhat different reaction. When the mayor of Netanya, a controversial public figure in the neighborhood, addressed the Mimuna celebration in Arod's public park, he was welcomed with a hubbub of jeering, heckling and booing. Both he and the disconcerted organizers were undeterred, and they perfunctorily completed their part in the festivities.

Indeed, the issue of the relationships between Arod and Netanya constantly preoccupy discussions and encounters among members of the project's staff. It is generally felt that the municipality of Netanya greatly benefits from the operation of the project in Arod because its services and functions relieve the former of its duties and obligations towards the latter. Years of neglect and disregard by the municipality engender a cumulative sense of acrimony and frustration among residents. Thus, members of staff maintain that in return for the neighborhood not being an extra drain on the resources of Netanya, the municipality should make special allowances to Arod by way of granting planning permits, approving local projects and giving a free hand to the Matnas in running the affairs of the neighborhood.

Such devolution of power is not always relished by residents who are aware of its inevitable consequence in expanding and strengthening the jurisdiction of the community and, in turn, reducing the ability of residents to negotiate terms with the authorities in protecting what they consider to be crucial interests. Thus paving a road through a residential area might be considered by the project to be of prime importance to the neighborhood, and as an undesirable nuisance by residents of the area. Cases of likewise nature arose in the steering committee when issues on the agenda are regarded as a boon by the project and as a bane by some resident representatives. The fact that municipality officials present at the meeting have the power to tip the balance is an added incentive to win their support. Thus, the potential intervention of local authorities in the relationships between residents and the project make for yet another dynamic factor deriving from the delineation of neighborhood boundaries.

Reciprocal relationships with the surrounding metropolis are, as illustrated by the previous case, based on the recognition of the "community" as a fairly autonomous, largely self-sufficient constituency, which at its bid can muster enough resources to claim an independent position regarding the daily running of neighborhood life. Evidently, municipally controlled matters such as water supply, street lighting, police protection, the sewer system and rubbish collection are not likely to be taken over by the project. Nevertheless, the efficacy of operating these services is indeed a negotiable issue, open to bargaining and manipulations. These are based on two aspects of the project: its self-containment and the services that it can offer to the municipality.

Such standing of relative independence vis-à-vis the local authority is granted to Arod through the massive flow of project resources into it. Because the major problems of housing and welfare are handled by sources other than town hall, the Matnas could consolidate its autonomy with regard to the municipality by strengthening its ties with the national project, and hence increase its dependency on it. Thus, neither autonomy nor dependency can be treated as absolute characteristics but must be seen in relation to a given frame of action and decision making and as interconnected, sometimes inversely-related phenomena. Indeed, in spheres that are directly germane to the municipal concerns, the project endeavors to sustain a high degree of independence. This might offer a complementary explanation to the emphasis put on cleanliness, physical safety and the protection of property—all are matters within the responsibility of local authority. Self-repair and restoration of damaged equipment and premises, a local civil guard unit and cleaning-up public sites are attempts in that direction. Conversely, issues under the auspices of either the Government or the Jewish Agency are left to the devices of those authorities. Such are the critical areas of employment and formal education, neither of which are regarded as the prime concern of the project.

The establishment of a mode of reciprocal relationships with Netanya is not confined to decreasing dependency, but also applied to local resources that can be of service to nonresidents. The prospective show-piece of the neighborhood—the new Matnas— is regarded as the major facility at the disposal of Arod that can be made available for the use of other boroughs at a price. Envisaged as a "country club" styled Matnas, it is thought to offer more than merely a wide range of amenities and activities. Its vision is of a marker of the transmutation of the neighborhood into a middle-class community with the ability to project this quality onto the outside world, and thereby qualify Arod to a redefinition of its image.

A more specific service along that vein is the modern, newly-built day crèche designed to cater to the needs of children of working mothers. Members of staff are convinced that the residents of Arod would not avail themselves to take full advantage of the facility, because most local working mothers would prefer to use kinship networks for the purpose of child-minding rather than a public service, however inexpensive it might prove to be. The anticipated partly-empty capacity of the crèche was, therefore, expected to be filled by other Netanya inhabitants who were assumed not to enjoy the caring support of extended families. The unsubsidized service would bring into the project welcome income and, at the same time, would help endorse Arod as an acceptable educational environment befitting the "first Israel" strata.

The attempt to transform Arod into a nondeprived neighborhood bearing the badges of a "first Israel" residential area does not necessarily entail dicarding the various ethnic heritages associated with the neighborhood. Conversely, rather than dispensing with traditional symbols and rituals, they are exploited as yet another resource in gaining recognition for its hospitality and centrality in Netanya's cultural life. This is particularly manifested in the organization of the Mimuna celebrations, which are held under the slogan "Arod invites Netanya." Unlike other Project Renewal neighborhoods, which chose to send large delegations to represent them in the central official festivities in Jerusalem, the Matnas of Arod decided that the occasion should be viewed as an opportunity for staging the significance of the neighborhood within the Netanya scene. It is an added testimony to the premium set by the project on the place of Arod in the town as against the marginality of publicity given to relations with other external elements. As stated before, this is not a reflection of the importance attached to Government or Jewish Agency authorities, but rather of the value of manipulability of community as a commodity ascribed to the event vis-à-vis the municipality, and with regard to the central project, the former being amenable to negotiation through such activities, whereas the latter was considered to be unaffected by the same.

Undoubtedly, the cultural legitimacy granted in recent years in Israel to political and other uses of ethnic elements is regarded by the Matnas as a license to incorporate stigmatizing aspects of "community" life into the construction of the Mimuna as a metaphor for neighborhood identity. However, when presentations of the Arod project are made outside the neighborhood, great care is taken to diffuse such events of any shred of ethnicity. Because such occasions are many and the Matnas does not spare an effort to encourage and even initiate participation in them, the consistency of neutralizing elements of undesirable connotation has been well established. In effect, it can be argued that whatever is acceptable as a symbol of community life inside the neighborhood was strictly forbidden outside it. Thus, those elements of the "community" that assume partial stigmatization internally, are meticulously eliminated externally. Far from generating a double standard, it is a dual manifestation of one view, which regards the outside as an arena from which recognition and legitimacy can be drawn and for which the project is accountable. The inside of neighborhood, however, is still a "community"-in-the-making, for which allowances should be made and latitude granted.

A myriad of activities represent the neighborhood outside and carry its name to a wide range of Israeli spheres of life and locations. First and foremost are sports competitions; second in reputation is the local youth movement, which won a few awards in the national march to Jerusalem, a well-publicized mass national event earning extensive coverage in the media; and last, are the shows of the pensioner's club. Both the sports coordinator and the youth organizer establish a power stronghold based on the prestige and significance of those "exported" community commodities.

It should be noted that those outside engagements are supposed to epitomize the spirit of a self-developed, self-generated community spirit of Arod, and as such are designed to be without a blemish of Project Renewal stigma. Hence their success is assessed in accordance with the extent to which they commensurate to the standards perceived by members of staff as typical of the "first Israel." Paradoxically, here the yardstick of self-sufficiency is directly related to the dependency on what is considered to be the desirable outside world. The reverse is the case of internal activities, which, although self-contained by nature, are regarded as conditioned by and, indeed, aimed at Arod's external environment.

The case of the local youth movement illustrates this last point. Being official representatives of Arod on a few nationwide events, the youth appear immaculately attired, carrying the neighborhood banners and integrating themselves into the other delegations. In Arod itself, however, they are treated as the young elite, which, although on the right road, still need nurturing and polishing. Furthermore, they are often assigned to observe, watch and eliminate stigmatic manifestations among other residents, such as unruly behavior, disturbances and neighborhood defacement.

An interrelated case in point is parents' expressed aspiration regarding their children's future. Although most parents consider the educational system in Arod to be adequate for their children's needs, they also conceive of those needs as being confined within the constraints of the neighborhood. In other words, a child who can "make it" out of Arod is regarded as exceeding the bounds of his capabilities and is therefore an exception that proves the rule, as it were. The "Israeli" oriented activities held in the neighborhood (see The "Israelization" of Arod, Chapter III, section IV) are therefore viewed as half-measured attempts that confer the participant with the insignia of extra-Arod identity, but that did not equip him to claim a full-fledged nonstigmatic status. It is that set of trappings that is employed in self-presentation outside the neighborhood. Speaking impeccable Hebrew, free of an ethnically identifiable accent, being attuned to current trends and fads, and fashioning habits and manners in line with the images projected by the media and town-life to which Arod's residents are exposed daily—all are seen as badges of assimilation that enabled people to adapt to the world outside the neighborhood, but not to be accepted or absorbed by it. As is argued in Chapter V, this state of hovering constitutes the life-line of the project.

Indeed, any infringement on that set of boundaries that is liable to upset the fragile balance between "in" and "out" poses a threat to the very foundation of the project and his has to be dealt with. Thus, students and academics who merely by their professional accomplishments break the limits of perennial transition are not expected to take active part in the running of the project, as they are considered to be beyond the world of residents. In fact, one of the arguments used at one time against the director referred to his academic qualifications as a possible hindrance in communicating with residents. He had, according to his contestant, already crossed the Rubicon of understanding and sympathy with the problems of the neighborhood. The other end of the same scale, that is, "problem-riddled" residents who are deemed to be unable to reach that state are, as discussed in Chapter III, regarded as welfare cases belonging to the domain of social work and therefore unfit for "community" life.

Other incongruous elements are residents of other deprived areas whose casual involvement with the Arod project is vociferously rejected. There are a few other neighborhoods in Netanya known for their relatively low socioeconomic standing, out of which the borough of Selah is the only other Project Renewal neighborhood. It is this fact that makes Selah both a competitor and a reference point for assessing the success and the achievements of the Arod project. It also serves as a bottom-line marker of deprivation and disarray. In comparison, Arod regards itself as being on a higher, more advanced footing. To maintain this valuable distance, a constant vigilance has to be kept to safeguard it against infiltration of undesirable Selah elements.

Thus, disorder and disturbance on an organized Matnas trip is imputed to the unwelcome participation of Selah residents because "our residents know how to behave." A purposed joint basketball delegation has never been formed and neither were shared summer schools. In fact on many occasions, members of staff are warned not to allow residents of the more underprivileged neighborhood to partake in Arod's functions. Visitors to Arod are often advised to pay a visit to Selah for the purpose of comparison. The geographical fact that Selah does not border with Arod and is situated in the opposite side of Netanya's outskirts makes for very little mingling anyway and thus, the image of Selah as the essence of impoverishment and disarray remains untampered by reality. It should be noted that the conceived deplorable state of that neighborhood is by no means regarded as a reflection on the project team responsible for it. Conversely, the staff is often praised for its incessant efforts in spite of residents' apathy and reluctance to be "regenerated" by the project.

If Selah and local welfare-stricken residents become untouchable by virtues of their menacing effect on community creation, some other entities within the neighborhood itself are considered to be too worthless and valueless for this ultimate objective. Thus those establishments that, although territorially located in the neighborhood, are not amenable to serve as community commodities nor are they likely to be incorporated into the project, are subject to disregard and preclusion from the scene set by the Matnas. Two noted examples can illustrate this phenomenon. The first is the religious technical high school that serves the population of Netanya and is viewed with ambivalence. Although a source of pride to the neighborhood for its high educational standards, the school is not quite regarded as a part of Arod because neither its staff nor most of its students are local residents. The school itself does not treat Arod as a special arena for its extra-curricular voluntary activities, but as a part of the "Netanya community," which is viewed by the headmaster as a target for the training cadre of "young leadership." The "commitment to the community" asserted by the school is therefore similar in nature to the patronizing pledges made by other extra-neighborhood public organizations.

The second case that demonstrates the insularity of the territorially Arod-based establishment concerns a geriatric center, one of the biggest in the country, situated right behind the premises of the temporary Matnas. The institution, a publicly run facility, could have attracted a multitude of "community" oriented activities such as voluntary help, joint functions with the able-bodied patients and shared recreational projects. Instead, the girded fence encircling the institutional enclosure has turned into an invisible barrier sequestering the place from any kind of Project Renewal involvement, of for that matter, from any association with residents. Despite the expressed wish of the center's welfare officer to establish links of cooperation with the neighborhood, no such scheme has materialized. This occurs even though many of the institution's work force came from Arod and despite the fact that the Matnas, from time to time, hires from some of the public amenities available at the center. The fact that the institution is neither a testimony of the neighborhood's self-sufficient accomplishments nor is it an exportable community commodity, makes its existence in the heart of Arod of no value to the project.

Turning "community" into a "social commodity" partly resolves the dilemma of dependent autonomy because it renders the idea of community, albeit with considerable limitations, dynamic and negotiable. At this point, the social world is infused with the vitality and thrust of a temporal entity.

NOTE

1. It would be instructive to compare the operation of bureaucratic agencies in a community-oriented setting, such as Arod, to pre-Project Renewal intervention schemes in Israeli deprived neighborhoods. Ethnographic material on the latter can be obtained in Marx (1976), Handelman (1976) and Lewis (1979). This last research is of particular interest because the studied town has recently been included in the project.

Chapter V

The Temporal Dilemma:
Permanency Versus Change

The process of a social world evolving from a sentiment-based domain into a structure of organized activities involves a fundamental contradiction between the imputed immutability of the object around which interest is centered and the dynamics of the social interaction generated by it. In the case of community, this schism can be described in terms of the relationship between various conceptions of the term and the respective modes of control implemented to reflect or to generate them.[1] It will be argued that each such mode of control reproduces a different temporal perspective and hence, the social world of community encapsulates a wide range of potential time-universes in accordance with the different social properties of the situations and contexts involved in its constitution.

Inherent in the ethos of Project Renewal is the teleological time perspective of a community-geared transformation. Yet, the organizational structure designed to induce such change is set within the time limits of the terminality of the project (see Deri 1983). Furthermore, structural factors, such as the variety of career trajectories pursued by those involved in running the project and the absence of employment opportunities offered to residents by it, play an important part in rendering the temporal framework of the project inextricably complex.

To disentangle this knotted mesh of temporal perspectives, it is necessary to ascertain the temporal properties of the social context in which the various protagonists in the social world of Arod's community operate. Conceptions of "community" vis-à-vis their respective advocates, therefore, are the focus of the following.

It is my contention that not only is the concept of community a socially manipulable construct employed in the service of various sets of interests and outlooks, but that the means and ways adopted to implement such pursuits are, to a large extent, hinged on a corresponding view of "community." This interplay between images and the behavioral patterns associated with them engenders some intriguing observations. First, there is a multitude of social constructions subsumed under the general term "community." More often than not, such variegated concepts stand in contradiction to one another in accordance with the different time perspectives that they are made to reflect and to reinforce.

Furthermore, it will be demonstrated how, in some cases, the measures to attain certain declared "community"-geared objectives can be incongruous with the fundamental theme instilled in and advocated by the same concept. In other words, the business of working out a certain conception of "community" is often contradictory to what that conception is deemed to represent. A significant implication deriving from such discrepancies draws on the delineation of internal boundaries within the neighborhood. It will be argued that distinctions made between and by various categories of residents are devised to befit needs and constraints arising from applying ambivalent criteria to suit various components of "community life."

Out of the almost infinite range of approaches to "community" prevailing in the neighborhood, four loci of activity concerning the topic of community are chosen to serve as pivotal foci for discussion in this section. The first is the Matnas; the second is the welfare and community services; the third consists of residents' positions and behaviors; and the fourth concentrates on structural aspects instilled in the project as a blueprint for "community." Needless to mention that each of these is in itself a conglomerate of different and changing views grouped and fused together merely for analytic convenience. The fourth dilemma therefore suggests that diverse community structures cannot, and indeed do not, converge to form a unified concept because they are based on contradictory temporal grounds.

Hence, to merely imply that the participants in the scene of the local Project Renewal do not have the courage of their convictions to follow a single coherent conception of community is both unjust and inaccurate. Rather, the following analysis suggests that in an intricate and complex context such as that, consistency and correspondence between worlds of action and spheres of imagery can hardly be expected or established.

Being caught up in a gripping reality of high-powered phraseology and unexplained uncontrollable forces, and lending themselves to be exposed to that influence, the people in question try to make the most of a confusing, sometimes self-contradictory milieu. The result clearly does not conform to systematic, logical mode of thinking—commonly expected from a bureaucratically administered setting. Our discussion of attempts to control "community," to bridle it to the worldview and interests of people, will be guided and governed by the temporal properties embedded in each such attempt.

I. THE CONTAINED COMMUNITY—
CONTROL THROUGH SPONTANEITY

The arduous effort spent on purging the Matnas team from any connotation of welfare work, an effort that includes the territorial separation of the two units and the reserved cooperation between them, produces a twofold result. The Matnas as an indentifiable center for neighborhood activities has to be constantly watched, lest its self-imposed image of a nonwelfare establishment is damaged or tarnished by diversion toward such matters. Hence, residents indeed recognize the Matnas premises as a local focus of organized functions; however, with the elimination of welfare services, it is hardly regarded as a community center. Residents, by complying with the stigma of a problem-afflicted area, equate community care with direct problem-solving orientation. Consequently, the team of the Matnas is faced with the self-imposed dilemma of reinforcing a community image devoid of the main attribute ascribed to it by residents.

The main course of action taken by Matnas Staff in handling the predicament is to institute as many established activities as possible to provide frameworks for generating "community"-geared symbolism. The entire panoply of those settings is listed in Chapter III; a closer look at some of them may shed some light on their place in constructing the Matnas as a community center. The guiding principle that governs the establishment of "community" facilities is that Arod is to become a self-contained environment, run and monitored by the social project. Thus the question of activities overlapping similarly designated functions held in Netanya or even in neighborhood-based settings is unconnected to the Matnas. The vernacular cultural autonomy claimed by the project is absolute and covers all Matnas-affected walks of life in the neighborhood. It is significant to note that within this context, "community" is often equated with popularly held conceptions of "culture," that is, modes of behavior implying good manners, educational pursuits, nonvulgar "civilized" recreational pastimes and typical middle-class entertainment. This equation enables the exclusion of welfare functions and the inclusion of images of nonstigmatic Israeli society.

Several Matnas-initiated local projects attest to this issue. There exists in Arod a small-scale entertainment group whose main material and repertoire consists of sketches and popular songs staged in a vaudeville-style presentation. The Matnas decided that the kind of entertainment offered by that group is not sufficiently respectable for Arod, and hence a local theater company has been set up with auditions, a hired director and plans for plays and shows in which pride can be taken. Drama as a "community" activity has been advocated and implemented in many Project Renewal neighborhoods, but Arod's theater, unlike similar set-ups in other localities, is not designed to put on mimetic performances of the reality in a neighborhood riddled with problems and plights. Rather, it is designated to operate as a proper theater company not pertaining to the status of Arod as an underprivileged area. Again, a pivotal cultural setting of community significance is divorced from any association to the welfare aspect of its surroundings.

Unlike the case of the local theater, which was aborted by lack of interest and shortage of suitable actors, the local youth movement proves to be a resounding success in terms of participation and of importance. Recruitment to the movement is directed at a wide age spectrum and the response is usually enthusiastic. Activities are held in public air-raid shelters and the coordinator, a Matnas worker, as well as the instructors are all Arod residents. Activities are, to a large extent, in the same vein as those typical of the Scouts, but involvement in local affairs is pronounced and prolific. Modeled on well-established Israeli youth movements, Arod's own version derives its proclaimed uniqueness and its self-justification not from the specific needs and problems of the neighborhood, but from the professed conviction that Arod possesses a defined identity that has to be reflected in its community institutions, of which the youth organization should be a feather in the project's cap.

As the nature and the characteristics of that peculiar quality has never been aired, the movement is lauded for representing a set of desirable values thought to be essential to community life. The picture of such a visionary community is a mosaic of "help," "consideration," "care" and "peace." None of these is qualified or applied as a given code of practice, nor are any specific expectations leveled at the youngsters.

This attitude dovetails a whole approach developed in the Matnas toward the meaning of "community." Apart from one constituent of community, all the other principles along which community should be constructed and brought into life are ill-defined and self-contradictory. The exception is the emphasis put on Jewish and national festivals and holidays. Such days are regarded as "the spirit and soul of the community" and are thus put on the pedestal of Matnas activities. Being a fusion between nonpoliticized ethnicity and identification with the state and the nation, such occasions are probably the one and only problem-free zone of "'community," and hence provided a readily-available uncomplicated stage for realizing that idea. The fact that, except for Independence Day and Remembrance Day preceding it, all the other holidays bear an undeniable mark of ethnicity and are celebrated in accordance with various customs and traditions does not seem to impinge on that view. Furthermore, such festivals, which are usually family-based events, can be seen as a threat to the dominance of the Matnas. Yet, such an eventuality is neither mentioned nor insinuated. The reason for this probably rests with the observation that as far as the project is concerned, the attainment of community is not necessarily connected to the residents' reality.

This is attested to by the recurrent theme of depicting the community as a living organism whose vitality and viability depended on its well-being, with the prominent assumption being that Arod is indeed a "healthy community," with the exception of a few marginal elements. Those elements, such as feckless welfare cases, criminals and unruly residents, are to be eliminated or, alternatively, ignored, if the community is to survive as a functioning body. Often, the term "their language" is used to refer to the appropriate approach that ought to be taken in dealing with residents whose presence in the neighborhood endangers the "fabric of community life." Thus, a clear demarcation line is drawn between "the community" and the outsiders from within who wish to wreck it. The distinction between "we" and "them" indicates that eradication rather than assimilation is thought to be the correct course of action applicable to such cases. Indeed, no rehabilitation scheme for Arod's imprisoned residents nor any programs for released convicts have been proposed. The main position is of general dissociation from the "contaminating elements" and taking a tough line with those who interfere with the operation of the Matnas. However, delinquent children and young offenders enjoy more leniency because they are not regarded as "hopeless cases," and thus are amenable and presumably receptive to the corrective treatment of the project. The handling of those children involves special personal tutoring given by Arod's resident students whose record as stigma-fighters qualifies them to set an example to the stigma-afflicted. Great pride is indeed taken in those young novices who display some degree of compliance with the expectation of the Matnas, and thereby disengage themselves from the detrimental influence of their own families. Phrases such as "although he comes from 'x' stock, his behavior is exemplary" or "you wouldn't guess his origin" are commonplace and typical of this attitude.

How then is a "healthy community" supposed to develop? What is the role assigned to project staff to induce its emergence? The ominous termination of the project in Arod does not allow for long-term plans to be devised, and thus the problem of how to generate a community without the building of its necessary edifice requires an answer that may commit the project to the idea of community as its prime concern, while exonerating it from any temporal commitment to the future. This seemingly inextricable dilemma is resolved by the advocacy of the notion of spontaneous involvement (for further discussion, see Moore and Myerhoff 1975).

Community is reduced to its "spirit," "soul" and "presence"— all of which are essential and none of which is replaceable. To transcend residents to this desirable sphere, members of staff are asked to invest their whole being in that enterprise. The final conquest, therefore, will be accomplished when that total immersion of staff to the idea impregnates the whole reality of the project. Such absolute and unbounded submergence might, in the end, initiate "a positive community process." This vision of the emergent community, eschatological though it is satisfies the need to envisage Arod as a community in progress. The Matnas is viewed in that context as the epochal drive that makes the process possible.

As intimated before, these sets of nebulous and mystified concepts with their quasi-religious twang and added ideological relish are aimed at members of staff rather than at residents. If the zeal and fervor are to be debunked, the use for such terminology can be viewed as a tactical ploy employed in an organization whose staff turnover is high and whose survival prospects are considered to be low.

For members of staff to be remiss is of much less consequence than for them to assume direct responsibility and vie for power and authority within the Matnas. Since no long-term reward system comprising of promotions and career opportunities can be introduced, any claim for power has to have immediate implications. Thus, to avert such potential threats, a set of ill-defined, vague and noncommital parameters for assessing success and evaluating progress is applied. The only renegade case of a defiant member of staff who has a substantial claim for power is that of the sports coordinator (see the previous chapter). It stands to prove the point in question, because he is the only member of staff who regards his involvement in the neighborhood as a long-term calculated career in which the Matnas plays an ephemeral part.

This interpretation accounts for the seemingly unbridgeable gap between the total obscurity of "community" jargon and the extremely business-like efficacy in which the project operates (see the previous chapter). Members of staff are expected to report promptly and accurately to their areas of responsibility. A close check is kept on attendance, on money collection and on the state of equipment and property. Although each member of staff is said to assume sole responsibility for the functions for which he or she is in charge, the tendency in the Matnas is to centralize the supervision over the wide range of dispersed activities held under its auspices in the neighborhood. Thus, the office with its administrative facilities, filing system, bursary, typing, photocopying and ticket distribution, and so forth, becomes an unavoidable venue frequented by workers whose specific assignments do not require the Matnas as a base.

This form of control becomes possible as a result of the role merger between the positions of head of the Matnas and director of the social project. It is interesting to note that the rationale for that combination is stated by the incumbent of that position as the need to "orchestrate activities and to avoid having two heads for the same project, a thing that can only cripple and disorganize our efforts. Order must be the order of the day it we are to succeed." The fact that that set of phrases is derived from a diametrically opposite domain to the "community" charged vocabulary is only too obvious, and opposite domain to the "community" charged vocabulary is only too obvious, and stands to cast a doubt on the validity of either, or else to attest to the relative applicability and flexibility of both within different contexts and situations.

II. THE HIDDEN COMMUNITY— CONTROL THROUGH PLANNING

This last point of differentially-conditioned situations and settings can be extended to cover the community-bound worlds of the other protagonists in the Arod scene. The social workers situated in the locality, although conforming to the basic tenants of renewal and revitalization, operated within an entirely different frame of reference to that of the Matnas. Being official members of the project team does not seem to prevent them from constituting another arena for their outlooks and activities. If the reasons responsible for this change of perspective are to be ascertained, a host of factors have to be considered. Ranging from long-term career prospects through pronounced professional commitment, to the pool of resources at their disposal and their target population, the dimension constructing the working reality of the social workers has little in common with the Matnas. In fact, rivalry and competition are more in place.

For all social workers (and for that matter, in accordance with the abovementioned set of criteria, the community worker belongs to that category) the idea of community is of prime importance, as it is to Matnas staff. However, unlike the latter, whose community is a thriving timeless vision, the social workers are in constant search for the "real" community.

Being preoccupied with "problem-stricken" residents, social workers often ascribe both the roots and the remedy for such conditions to the state of the community. Conceptions of maladjustment to the existing community are mixed with counter-concepts of building or modifying the community to create the ambiguous reality of that idea. If community is in existence, then maladjustment to it can provide an explanation to a whole range of problems; but if community is in a state of dereliction and disarray, adaptability to its shaky structure would merely keep residents at bay from the desirable goal of good functioning. In either case, the concept can be and, indeed, often is manipulated to befit changing professional exigencies, but neither construction is put into question. Thus, although the content and the structure of the aspired community remains blurred and ill-defined, the reality of a community as a viable entity to be reckoned with seems to be self-evident. Consequently, social workers engage in a perpetual two-pronged task of searching for existing rudiments of community coupled with an attempt to generate and create one.[2]

Because discovering a dubious entity can amount to its invention, the search for Arod's communal potentialities turns to be the making of it. Talk of "community awareness" and "collective responsibility" is forged into some concrete form, such as the school for public activists, the information unit and the preparation for the local election campaign—all organized and supervised by the community worker. If the information unit is designed to mold the profile of Arod in facts and figures, the elections and the school are regarded as tools for the revitalization of community leadership. The concept attached to these enterprises is that once residents are relieved from the burden of old allegiances and break away from outdated loyalties, the well-hidden foundation of community spirit will be unearthed.

Meetings with residents to induce more interest and participation in community affairs are to no avail, and attempts to turn school committees and parents' associations into centers of community activities yield no results. Nevertheless, social workers maintain that only through the rise of a grass-roots consciousness can a claim for community power-sharing evolve.

It is this last point that invokes the meaning behind that seemingly professional conviction. In the power struggle over the mastery of local resources and the coverage of fields of influence in the neighborhood, winning over residents is a crucial issue. It is shown how the Matnas manages to neutralize residents' participation and that that apparent Achille's heel is picked up as a target for both structure and recruitment. The insistence that the project is accountable to the residents whose hour will come to demand a satisfactory explanation for their exclusion from the core of decision making is used to undermine the claim for absolute authority and indisputable success made by the project's leaders. Social workers therefore, argue that their direct involvement with residents and their close acquaintance with their problems qualifies them more than anybody else to claim a knowledge of the community and to use it to the benefit of its inhabitants.

To realize this asset, the social workers have to phase out the previous notion of the community and to safeguard their control over the newly-acquired information. Because most of the data gathered in the information unit is obtained, monitored and circulated by the community worker, this objective is attained, but only as much as that material is really needed and used. The redrawing of internal boundaries within the neighborhood in the course of the election campaign, administrative and bureaucratic as it was, was aimed to reinforce that goal on a much larger more significant scale. Arod A, B and C (see Chapter II) are traditionally identified with certain ethnic groups, kinship networks and socioeconomic local stratification. By convincing the legal bodies in charge of the election and the old neighborhood committee to agree to cast aside the old ethnically-based divisions in favor of a new redelineation of election zones, the community worker instills new terms of reference for the redistribution of power in Arod.

The principle of the redelineation is to obtain a proportional representation system in three equally populated areas and thus do away with the old system, which was based on a gross disproportion between Arod A, B and C, a situation that perpetuated the reign of the old leadership. An alignment of interest between the Matnas, the community worker and many residents, coupled with the poor resistance of the old committee, enabled this move to materialize.

Thus, a new "community" structure is created. This is of no immediate consequence to the Matnas, but might have significant implications in the future, for if the project is terminated, the plan to redivide Arod can affect any redistribution of resources and any emergent allocation of power and prospective leadership. In any case, the social workers are there to stay and for them the new community frame can prove to be more manipulable than the previous state.

III.   THE RELUCTANT COMMUNITY—
CONTROL THROUGH NEGOTIATION

Bombarded with community-laden ambivalent messages, the clients of the neighborhood services, that is, the residents, view this newly-introduced commodity askance. Although any monolithic portrayal of residents' responses would be misleadingly inaccurate, a certain pattern of behavior emerges in the neighborhood to justify some broad, but nevertheless reserved, generalizations. At the heart of such characterization stands the observation that even though awareness of the concept is ample among residents, attempts to understand and to grapple with its intricacies are scant. Rather, as most residents realize, the significance attached to "community" by almost all members of staff, be it Matnas or social workers or even local activists, the trademark of "community" is often treated as negotiable. Residents who take advantage of the range of services and benefits offered to them by the project are quite willing to pay the price of wearing the guise of community.

However, when not exposed to such expectations or when performing as community-motivated subjects can be detrimental to vested interests and enshrined images, such behavior is liable to swift transformation. Thus, residents appear, on selective occasions, to treat community exerted pressures as threats to be resisted.[3]

The overall residents' prevalent view of community consists of elements not necessarily congruous with any of the aforementioned perspectives. For most residents, the community is represented in the physical layout of the neighborhood and the socioeconomic well-being of its inhabitants. Community work, therefore, is conceived of as the obligation of the various agencies in the neighborhood to improve housing conditions and to deal with problems of delinquency, employment, education and the provision and care of essential amenities, such as the sewer system and the collection of rubbish. The idea of a community as a manifestation of some kind of collective consciousness is remote and incomprehensible to residents. In fact, if a sound conception of community were to be detected at all among residents, it would consist of people and their everyday concerns such as means of livelihood, accommodation and manageable environment.

Thus, most residents do not equate community with "culture" nor do they dwell on the past or plan for the future in order to explore it. Conversely, residents resent what they consider to be an over-generous spending on "cultural activities," which are, as one resident said, "superfluous to our life here." Furthermore, many residents stress that out of the variety of cultural events that were available in Netanya, they are inclined to attend very few, least of all theater productions and courses of study. Fun in the form of light entertainment and subsidized trips is welcome but not in excess because, as one resident states, "the money could be put to 'better use.'" Such critical remarks questioning the appropriations of project funds are commonplace in the neighborhood, although, with the exception of the local opposition, no public or even individual protest has ever been raised.

Dealing with municipal authorities, housing officials and welfare services seems to constitute the main roles ascribed to the Matnas by residents. However, the young as well as the old, who are more directly involved in project functions, develop different expectations. Being unconcerned, as yet, with housing and welfare problems, the young do identify the Matnas with socially-geared activities to which they are drawn. The elderly, on the other hand, who are perceived to have social problems such as loneliness and alienation, are introduced to the Matnas through its special programs for the aged, such as study groups and pensioners' clubs.

Awareness of the existence of the project is acute as far as practical services, such as summer schools for children and their mothers, or library facilities, are concerned. It is gradually dimmed with the decreasing pragmatic value placed on a given service. Thus, although lectures and even "cultural" entertainment are not well received, the *Tehila* program for adult education (see Chapter II) is in great demand. The reason is that most of the participants, usually mothers of school children, rejoice at the opportunity to be able to familiarize themselves with some of the school material of their children and thus help them with their homework and follow their academic achievements and enjoy an improved image in the eyes of their offspring.

All this evidence attests to the observation that the "community" boundaries prescribed by various members of staff are not observed by residents. Neither external boundaries circumscribing the neighborhood as a social enclave, nor internal borders dividing people according to imputed problems and needs are applicable to the manner by which residents relate to other residents and to nonresidents. In fact, that division between "in" and "out" does not impinge on the construction of social life in Arod, because being a resident of the neighborhood had very little bearing on one's self-image and identity. Rather, the ties and connections that count are anchored in people's places of work and mainly in kinship networks, both of which extend far beyond the geographical borders of the neighborhood.

Kinship ties are faithfully nurtured with both outside relations and kin residents. Mutual visits are regularly and frequently paid and most Saturday excursions outside the neighborhood are devoted to maintaining such contacts. For most residents, these ties seem to constitute the core of their social life, although suggestions of *Hamulot*-formation, that is, structures of extended family network, are rejected outright as being anachronistic residuals of past traditions. Apart from serving a destigmatization function, this renunciation of fixed-bind'ng kinship units indicates a sense of exercising free choice in selecting desirable relationships from the available pool of family members. The fact that kinship ties are scattered around a wide geographical area and, that owing to the economic structure of Israel, their operation as corporate groups is not even potentially feasible, prevents them from being centers for social control in any significant sense. Yet, labile and noncommittal as they are, family obligations and loyalties are not given to be superseded by forms of community attachments.

The limits of complying with community impositions can be transpired, as demonstrated by the two following examples. The first concerns a summer school run by the Matnas and organized on the basis of age-structure and assignated group symbols. The participants, Arod's school children, are only too eager to break down this form of organization and regroup themselves according to well-established kinship ties. The second case is associated with the local outcry regarding drug offences in the neighborhood. It is commonly accepted in Arod that such criminal activities mar the good name of the neighborhood and imperil the lives and the future of many of its young. Yet, any attempt to locate and detain the perpetrators of such acts is aborted by a response of furtive silence and lack of cooperation on the part of residents. Despite incessant calls by members of project staff, to "rid the community of such destructive elements," the "community" remains inattentive. As was well observed by the sports coordinator, whose involvement with residents is deep and direct, the reason for this is neither lack of interest nor fear. It is the fact that most offenders have strong family bonds in the neighborhood. Their protection and cover up, reluctant as these may be offered, is essential for their safety. Police opinion on the matter confirms this description.

Hence, with employment, crime, education and housing excluded from the social project operation, there are very few common denominators between the idea of community as advocated by staff and the community of people as conceived by residents. Incorporated into their everyday lives as yet more raw material for the construction of reality, the concept of community becomes part and parcel of the temporal flow constituting the negotiated social order in the neighborhood.

IV. THE SELF-SUBVERSIVE COMMUNITY— CONTROL DENIED

Searching for a suitable metaphoric analogy, the project director once equated community sentiments to Judaism and Zionism, meaning that the former should be elevated to the level of ultimate importance. Without attempting to fathom the profundity or the validity of that observation, it can be safely argued that it is an unequivocal assertion of the director's view of the cardinal place occupied by community in people's lives. But if the concept of community and its implementation is, as hitherto analysed, an incoherent, incongruous assemblage of outlooks, ideologies, policies and interests constantly conditioned and shaped by changing circumstances and contexts, what are the practical and structural implications of ascribing to a neighborhood the attribute of a community?

Notwithstanding the fact that all folk-definitions and views of community are subject to variegated situations and constraints, there is nevertheless one common denominator, low as it may be, which is present in all the perspectives described in the previous sections. This is the assumption that a designated group of individuals share some collective characteristics and hence, can be expected to build around it a meaningful social milieu distinguishing them from other groups of people. Had it not been for the impact of the concept of decision-making processes that shape the destiny of the people in question, it would have been merely a scholastic exercise to further discuss a construct whose foundation in reality and objective viability are dubious. However, man-made, manipulable and intangible as it is, the concept of community becomes an omnipresent phenomenon in the reality of Arod, and as such cannot be dismissed altogether as an insignificant figment of bureaucratic imagination or as a flight of ideological fancy smothered by good intentions and vested interests.

For the residents of Arod, being made into a community might entail far-reaching implications, of which the most ominous is the perpetuating of dependency on the authorities that devise and run that community. By forming a bureaucratically defined social enclave, receiving especially appropriated resources and enjoying a wide range of subsidized services and facilities, the administrators of the project provide the necessary prerequisites for spiralling dependency on their decisions. Simple and self-evident as this might appear, the argument requires further support and clarification.

To begin, it should be noted that the level and standard of services and amenities offered by the project is well above the residents' affordable income. Irrespective of cultural preference, the free, nonsubsidized market of computer clubs, theater shows, summer schools and psychological counselling offers such services at a price well beyond the limits of Arod's residents' economic position. Furthermore, as the project is not designed to cater to problems of occupational training and employment opportunities,[4] the likelihood of residents' financial means meeting the real cost of the facilities they use is very slim indeed. Thus, by making the symbols of an aspiring middle-class socioeconomic strata readily available and procurable, the project nurtures standards of living and expectation without a sound economic backing to guarantee their future fulfillment outside the sheltered "community." The extent of dependency, therefore, is a direct function of the width of the gap between income and services compared with opportunities and prospects outside the realm of the project. Because the level of the average income in Arod is not at the bottom of the scale, the living conditions are considered to be reasonable, and the proximity to the center of town makes for further convenience, the added facilities provided by the project increases its desirability as a residential area capable of attracting newcomers. Indeed, the rising value of property in the area proves this expectation. Thus, the idea of Arod being a community can take the form of a centrally administered protectorate sustained by residents bound to its confines by irresistible economic privileges.

If this is indeed the case, the question to be raised concerns the manner by which such a degree of dependency becomes acceptable to residents. Rather than presumptuously delving into residents' minds and toying with self-images, a viable vantage point for discussion can be found in reference to a literary piece serving as reading material for the women students of the adult education program, *Tehila*. This is a short children's story usually designated for kindergarten classes. The tale, entitled "The Disguised Egg" describes the adventures of a change-seeking egg in a constantly frustrating pursuit of a suitable metamorphosis in its identity. Having disguised itself as a whole range of similarly shaped objects and being snubbed and rejected by all of them, the disenchanted, yet experienced egg, resigns itself to the fact of its egginess and decides to return, without harboring any further illusory aspirations, to its original form to hatch and, hence be transformed into a chicken.

The analyses offered by the students to the meaning of the story clearly suggest that the message conveyed to most of them, and which appealed to their worldview, is the apparent fatalistic acceptance of one's position, condition and destiny in life. This is by no means an indication of the dismissal of personal abilities and desires, but it does imply that prospects of change and advancement are, to a considerable extent, determined by force of circumstance and lie within the limits of an inexorable environment. Thus, the individual's fate is shaped by constraints beyond his control, and hence are no reflection of his potential capabilities. The transformation of stigma into fate and of deprivation into innocuous necessity is a theme running through a great many residents' deliberations on their reality. The only area providing an arena for a worthwhile dispute and sufficient motivation to stage a protest in an attempt to change matters is the allocation of housing resources. There, the sense of injustice in the face of perceived favoritism is poignant. However, equity is never sought in comparison with the good fortunes of the out-neighborhood world. The multiethnic composition of Arod, coupled with residents' exposure to employment opportunities in other areas, aborts any attempt to generate a sense of being an oppressed minority and abated any accusation of discrimination.

In an insidious way, it is the openness of Arod, with its flimsy boundaries and the free mobility of its residents, that can be held responsible for reinforcing and bolstering the dependent "community," which eventually might set up such rigid borders around itself. Lack of awareness, complete with no acrimony or frustration, can put residents off guard to lend themselves to a self-perpetuating state of dependency.

A community of that nature may provide a limited sense of security, but through its complex system of allocating benefits and distributing privileges would regulate contacts with its self-imposed "outside world" and govern the lives of its residents in a manner totally unfit to the way of life outside it. The unconditional and absolute commitment in all walks of life that such a "community" might demand stands in sharp contrast to the separate, segmentary life worlds that characterize individual existence in a complex society. Thus community identity, when it gets out of hand, can prove to be the very barrier between the neighborhood and its social surroundings that the project has pledged to remove.

The accentuated sense of a different time and a different place already exists among some residents and members of the project staff. Not only can it be self-defeating for the project, but might also, owing to the increasing centralization of the project, trigger a process of politicizing the dependency. The possible consequences of this are beyond the scope of this discussion. However, rudimentary phenomena in this direction can be detected in the claims for power within the municipality and in some party-political maneuvering during the election campaign. Although this is well contained, the incipient potentialities are there and can yield results if patiently cultivated. Thus, however tenuous the political ties and pressures are now, the eventuality of Arod becoming a politically controlled enclave, not despite but because of its qualities as a "community," is not as inconceivable and remote as some residents would like to think.

The very behavior of residents with regard to the present dependency on authorities lends itself to be construed as a presage of events to come. Because the local project is conceived of as being devoid of any effective power on matters of prime importance such as education and employment, most residents view its operation as having no direct bearing on their future prospects. It is for this reason that, by and large, residents do not express conscious dependency on the project, and hence do not find it necessary or useful to enter into lengthy negotiating transactions with its officials. Characteristic of this is the lack of awareness of the connection between the project and the Government and the Jewish Agency. For many residents, the project is an autonomous body loosely associated with world Jewry and vaguely influenced by "Jerusalem"—a generalized mystification indicating some central administration. Hence, when issues of major concern, such as education and employment, are at stake, government ministries, rather than the local project, are charged with responsibility. Resentment and incrimination, therefore, are levelled at the omnipotent images of the indomitable forces behind the scenes of government. The exoneration of the local project from any responsibility and the perceived split between Arod's affairs and decisions taken in high places, forebode that, in the event of the project being a proxy of central government, the link between the two might be overlooked, thus enabling the latter to impose its will through the former with impunity.

The local image of the relationship with the "sister community" can illustrate a further aspect of the bond of uncontrollable dependency. Here, no mighty bureaucracy nor local authorities are involved and yet, the general attitude of residents is of deferential compliance with the power of the American benefactor who can withdraw his support at will and thus bring the project to an untimely end; hence the feeling of being at the arbitrary mercy of a charitable patron. Although hospitality, respect and information invested into the relationship are valued as essential in maintaining contact with New Jersey, it is by no means regarded as a sufficient safeguard against unpredictable breach.

With the imminent termination of the project, the unstable demographic structure of the neighborhood and the nebulous future support from abroad, the extent of uncertainty and insecurity is somewhat assuaged by the rugged solidity of durable and immutable dependency on central government. In that respect, a prospective transformation into a politicized "community" might not prove to be an abhorrent proposition to residents after all.

If the issue of residents' participation in the "community" is to be addressed, it is essential to consider several aspects of the connection between the social boundaries within which residents operate and the extent of commitment and interest displayed by them in involvement with the project. Because "community," as well as its boundaries, have already been analyzed as equivocally complex phenomena, and as the level of residents' participation has been established to be low, the point in question should refer to the reasons behind these observations, rather than to the adducement of further evidence.

The four dilemmas that constitute the main body of the presentation of Arod's self-contradictory "community" enterprise can be construed as a set of forces, which together construct the arena in which the boundaries of the reality of residents' involvement with the project is shaped.

Each of the dilemmas consists of two opposing themes, which combined with the other contradictions, generate a series of problems to which solutions are sought in the modes of behaviors and patterns of images described in the relevant sections. Thus, the neighborhood-conditioned dilemmas and their specific responses adopted by participants—residents and staff alike—engender a structure of ambiguities and ambivalences peculiar to the context and circumstances of Arod. Any behavior contingent on those parameters, and any resident enmeshed in them, can be thought to be within the boundaries of the constraints and incentives of that social entity. Conversely, perceptions and interactions that escape being caught up within the confluence of those dimensions of "community" life are, for all intents and purposes, outside its boundaries.

Involvement clamped by stigma, autonomy stifled by intervention, neighborhood subverted by residents, continuity defeated by termination and vice versa, manufacture a vicious circle of reactions and counterreactions anchoring the actor—be it a "resident" or a member of project staff—into the set of rules organizing the particular structure of that milieu.

This by no means suggests that every participant in the Arod scene is bound to be plagued by problems of incongruous reality and fractured identity. In fact, no participant abandons himself to the full impact of the host of factors embedded in the project. Some are completely disengaged from it to the extent that no sphere of their lives is tangent to the world of the Matnas and its surroundings. The very affluent seek their social circles and foster aspiration outside the neighborhood, while the very poor retain their dependency on the state welfare services regardless of the "community." Others resigned themselves to a small-scale selective involvement, and a few—mainly a few of members of staff and a handful of activists—are submerged in full-fledged participation.

As such, near-total immersion can mean a retreat from other areas of interest and relevance and an entanglement in a self-defeating pursuit of unattainable objectives. The temptations put by the project are easy to resist and its challenges remain unmet.

Thus, suggestions of remedial action and reorganization such as have been made on numerous occasions are not only impractical, but also ill-conceived and misguided. Lack of coordination, unaccomplished projects and low participation are not the fruit of inefficiency and mismanagement, but the inevitable consequence of various incompatible sets of attachments, connections and allegiances around which participants' lives are centered.

Different members of staff feel accountable to different foci of power and influence from which they respectively derived images and resources to construct their separate realities; residents are accountable to various extents to family, employment, friends, and so on. They also form their own interdependent small changable nuclei of accountability, which determine their willingness, interest and motivations to partake in the project. Therefore, it is almost self-evident that the attempt to pour together a mixture of distinctly different sets of accountability into a melting pot of a "community" simmering on the fire of "residents' participation" is doomed to be a logical fallacy as well as a practical pitfall.

Ensnared in a web of phantom concepts and mock realities, residents of Arod, particularly the ones whose keen interest in public affairs find no vent for its realization, have no alternative but to venture out of the neighborhood. With no real promise of progress and reward in an out-of-time, out-of-place encapsulated "community," some residents set forth to pursue a more rewarding course of involvement in the political arena of either the municipal authority or the national parties. Participation in the neighborhood project is considered to be a respectable preoccupation for those in search of ritualistic veneration and self-glorification, but hardly a worthwhile cause for long-term commitment and a spring-board for further advancement. It remains to be seen whether the winding down of the project will terminate the state of euphoric community for those participants, or if it is a case where structural dependency espoused to terminology of autonomy may render the social world of community in Arod self-perpetual.

NOTES

1. The approach to time implicit in our analysis subscribes neither to the concept of time as a conceptualization of change, such as in time-reckoning systems (see Maxwell 1972), nor to the scheduling perspective (see Roth 1962; Zerubavel 1981). Rather, it draws on the assumption that unlike chronological time, social time is a factor in its own right and its properties of multidimensionality, inconsistency and manipulability distinguish it from mere change (see Lauer 1981; Hazan 1985).

2. "Community dreams" in the form of future visionary communal institutions can be found in much of the community-oriented welfare literature. See, for example, Berkovitz (1984).

3. This view of relationships within the community probably constitutes the predominant approach in sociological research on the subject. This should be pointed out to emphasize the proximity in terms between the residents' "accomplishment" of community and the prevalent analytic paradigms.

4. This fact is acknowledged by the evaluating community of the project with the predicted consequence that, "the achievements of the project are endangered not only by the limitation placed on it, but even more by the current severe economic crisis. The people living in Project Renewal neighborhoods are most at risk in periods of unemployment and are most dependent on government assistance, which is now being reduced. Despite the gains they may have made under Project Renewal, their problems will be severe in the coming period" (The International Committee for the Evaluation of Project Renewal 1984, p. 71).

Chapter VI

The Rhetorics of Community: Boundaries and Accountability

The constraints embedded in the aforementioned dilemmas seem to constitute a vicious circle of structurally delineated community boundaries. It would appear that the determinancy of forces beyond residents' control has an unavoidable impact on the neighborhood. This impression is reinforced through its imprint in some of the written and verbal outputs communicated to the extra-neighborhood environments and emphasizing the "uniqueness" and inimitability of Arod. This rhetorical production of community contributes a great deal toward the process of sequestrating the neighborhood as a distinct social enclave from its surroundings. However, if our assumption that the descriptive activities focusing around the concept of "community" generate a community-couched social world, it would be plausible to expect that the open-ended dynamics of this behavioral construction will transcend structural constraints and contextual exigencies. That is, the rhetoric of community, by virtue of its own autonomous nature, gathers momentum beyond the limits of environmental conditions. It is, therefore, argued that a discrepancy might arise between the actual formation of a socially defined unit, flow of resources and local interests, on the one hand, and the fluidity, flexibility and rules of the descriptive activity pertaining to that unit, on the other hand.

Being an open system of communication, social worlds tend to reach out to other social domains, interweave with any tangent referential scope and flow freely through readily available symbolic channels. This diffusive permeability stands in apparent contradiction to some tenets of conventional wisdom and practical assumptions regarding community as a boundary-bound social context. Be it symbolic, bureaucratic, territorial or temporal, the principle of delineation is always challenged by competing modes of social organization. The social worlds generated in any milieu of communication transmit symbolic codes, cultural themes and social dilemmas across distinguishable arenas of action and irrespective of conflicting interests and incongruous realms of content. It is this inconsistency built into the relations between the notion of social worlds and the structural constraints within which such worlds emerge that this chapter sets to unfold. Predicated on the premise that rhetorical practices are amenable to sociological analysis in their own right and viable to the understanding of both verbal and nonverbal communication, the three following sections will respectively refer to descriptive, practical and ceremonial facets of community rhetorics. The assumption underlying the discussions is that issues of boundaries and accountability are evinced, articulated and resolved through the rhetorical production and reproduction of community imagery.

The pool of media records employed as sources for the rhetorics of community consists of local newspapers, billboard notices, official documents, transcripts of speeches and participant observation in neighborhood public events. It should be noted that for the purpose of this chapter, no analytic distinction is offered to discern between verbal phrases, visual images, printed matter and acting performance. It would seem that no substantive objective can be served by such exercise and that the practical exposure to community rhetorics is often an undistinguishable experience.

The following sections differentiate between three forms of asserting the idea of community. The first reflects rhetorical acts of depiction portraying the neighborhood as a community; the second is couched in declared practices creating and sustaining community life in the neighborhood; and the third is furnished by a publicity-performed symbolic representation of community. All three forms can be said to endow the notion of community with a tangible element.

I. DESCRIPTIVE RHETORIC

Above the caption: "The pictures speak for themselves," two photographs of two public waste-disposal units are printed in one of the issues of the local newspaper. The first shows an untidy, neglected unit littered with uncollected refuse, while the other depicts a neatly sealed, uncluttered unit. Encapsulated in this visible opposition is the notion of what the neighborhood is, and to some extent, is set—against the desirable, craved-for stage of the ideal community. The fact that dirt serves as a carrier for the message is no coincidence. As indicated before, cleanliness and hygiene have become a core symbol for the should-be, would-be community, and the association between the state of rubbish disposal and the stage of Arod as a community is thrown into relief in that wordless photographic image.

Contrasts and oppositions are employed not only to distinguish between reality and ideal past and present on "right" and "wrong," but also to reinforce the "community" and the "neighborhood." An analysis of two documents describing the changes in Arod in the course of the projects' operation might attest to this dichotomy. The first document, which was prepared by the direction of the local social project, is designated to promote Arod's case with the administration of the national project. It is titled "Five Years Later—Transformations in Arod" and highlights the main changes in the "community."

> We witness the creation of a creative community; enterprizing and involved and participating in unprecedented action while utilizing ample opportunities which are expressed in the blueprints for projects whose reputation reaches the town and its surroundings.

Having detailed some noticeable improvements in the distribution of welfare services, the setting up of local foci for social activities, changes of residents' behavior in public and the development of networks of communication within the community the author of the report sums up:

> There is no doubt that this collection of evidence is salient and stands to prove that a serious transformation has taken place through a transition

from the era of "give me," "I deserve it" to the era of "what I, the resident, can give?"

This statement is followed by a full description of various "cultural" and "educational" activities organized by the project for the residents. Hardly any mention is made of socioeconomic factors, or indeed, of any aspect pertaining to everyday living conditions. These constitute the main concern of the second document whose author—an official of the national project—fails to refer to "community" at all and instead employs the term "neighborhood" as its key descriptive objective.

This aridly phrased document, titled *The Population of the Arod Neighborhood—Main Characteristics* is replete with figures and tables purporting to accurately reflect the statistical parameters of the neighborhood. In a nonevaluative jargon, the report, while focusing on data of household size, levels of income and education and ownership of property, maintains that Arod has been characterized by a high degree of demographic stability and a still relatively low standard of living. Communal targets are amiss and social properties of the neighborhood are disregarded. Arod, therefore, is viewed as a demographically and territorially circumscribed neighborhood rather than as an amorphically defined community. A testimony to this difference is the absence of any reference to concrete community symbols such as the local Matnas and the activities of the social project.

Evidently, the differences in the nature of the two descriptive procedures are rooted in the diverse systems of accountability that frame each document. While the latter is couched in the nationwide administration and distribution of project-renewal resources, the former spells local interests and vernacular identity. To pursue this goal, comparative references must be overlooked while the inimitable uniqueness of the Arod community has to be emphatically stated.

Indeed, in an interview with the project director, the pronouncement that "Arod is one in its generation" is made alongside a photograph of newspapers clips describing Arod as being "at the vanguard of the computer era in the town." This theme is punctuated in the self-told life history of the project director who, in another interview, interlinks his personal conversion from a stigma-afflicted socially-underprivileged immigrant to Israel into a full-fledged respectable Israeli citizen whose idiosyncratic change of fate is interwoven into the unique transformation of the deprived neighborhood into a thriving, destigmatized community. The business of transition is subsequently described as "working on the foundation, not on nonsense," "uprooting the past" or simply, "renewal."

What is the significance of the distinction between "neighborhood" and "community" and what is the reason for the almost exclusive use of the latter term within the local project? It would seem that as already suggested, the social world of community, by transcending structural boundaries, facilitates and induces communication within a broader social scope and hence opens up new channels of exchange and explores novel possibilities and opportunities. The following discussion is concerned with such encroachments and centers on the ever-increasing circles of communicating the idea of Arod as a community into the spheres of the American Diaspora, the municipality and the state.

Spreading, expanding and variegating the scope of boundaries are not just emergent properties of the dynamics of a fluid social world. They function as practical responses to the dependency of the local project on the central administration. As the commitment to a sole system of accountability restricts the negotiating capacity of the neighborhood, the fostering of alternative arenas of action and resources becomes a prime concern for the local leaders. Such enhancement, particularly with respect to the sponsoring community in America, is to safeguard continuous financial support and to maintain a position of power within the municipal arena. The descriptive practices employed to sustain and furnish this aim are the subject of the following discussion.

Surrounding the inaugural ceremony of the new Matnas (see section III of this chapter), a multitude of descriptive activities mushroomed in the neighborhood. Following the event, the local newspaper published numerous photographs capturing memorable moments, such as the cutting of the tape at the opening, the fixing of *mezuzzot* (a Jewish custom of placing encased parchment scrolls containing scriptural texts onto the door-post) and the frolic nailing of plaques dedicating the various rooms to the names of the donors. All these photographs depicted guest members of the

American "sister community" intermingling with local
politicians and dignitaries, holding Torah scrolls or especially
posing for their photographs.

> Two miles south of the city of Netanya—forty minutes drive from
> Tel Aviv—the neighborhood of Arod, with 6,500 inhabitants, has
> long been regarded a symbol of "deprivation."
>
> Like other "underprivileged" neighborhoods in or on the
> outskirts of major Israeli cities, its community development and
> organization were not cohesive and mature enough to counteract
> the social problems of its immigrant population. Despite work done
> over the years by teachers, social workers, youth leaders, sports
> instructors and others, and a gradually improved standard of living,
> the neighborhood remained stigmatized, largely due to overcrowded
> housing, high delinquency and crime rates, and lack of both
> assertive and skilled Communal Leadership, and a sense of
> reputable self-image.
>
> Project Renewal set out to tackle these problems through linking
> the neighborhood with a well-established and committed Jewish
> community abroad, the infusion of funds and the mobilization of
> local resources and motivation for change. Among those most
> intensely involved in this process, as Chairman of the Project
> Renewal Committee in the United Jewish Community of B, is Dr.
> A., a dentist with a second home at Netanya, where he spends two
> months each summer with his family.

Question: Do you consider the relationship between the two
communities as a partnership between equals—with each side
contributing its share to the success of the project?

Dr. A: Differences between the two communities notwithstanding, our view has been and remains that each community should
contribute what it is best at doing. We in B know our job; we have
the capacity and the will to raise funds and to give you at Arod
the tools. Arod's neighborhood renewal team and residents council
must decide how to use these funds and put in the planning and
application that reflect local needs and requirements. At the same
time, genuine links and partnerships have begun to flourish on a
person to person and family to family basis over the years, and these
relationships must be extended.

Question: Do you recall instances in which B leaders and representatives suggested alternative uses for the funds raised and transmitted to Arod?

Dr. A: In all cases, we accepted the decisions made by the local project director and residents' representatives. We did advise that the auditorium of the new community center remain a multi-use open space, rather than have fixed seating. Our views were not accepted. We also thought that a sports field would be preferable to a closed indoor facility, gymnasium and sports hall. Again, we abided by the neighborhood director's choice of an indoor hall. Even if these decisions prove to be mistakes, the process of renewal includes taking choices and sometimes making mistakes.

Question: What considerations led you to recommend and accept the community center as the main component of the renewal project in Arod?

Dr. A: Our Board's policy was to enter a renewal project on condition that it had a construction program, so that Arod's needs and our requirements fitted. The ratio we eventually worked out— approximately one-third of the budget for social programs and two-thirds of the funds for new buildings, particularly the community center, struck a good balance in our view. Additionally, the community center hall, serving as an auditorium for the population of Netanya at large, can contribute a great deal to Arod's residents in the sense of breaking the cycle of social isolation and stigmatization of the past. If people come to Arod for a performance and realize that the neighborhood is an integral part of the city, a major objective of Project Renewal will be achieved.

Question: In what ways do you see the personal involvement of B residents increasing and the link with Arod residents becoming stronger?

Dr. A: A number of ways, through special continuation projects. Our youth sent a group to Arod for a summer visit last year. The program must be built better for it to succeed. Five hundred visitors from B have been in Arod, and enjoyed home hospitality with neighborhood families. Other, additional ideas must be tried out, and the bridge will become ever stronger through the living links we establish and maintain.

Evidently, the language of community that dominates the interview provides the rationale and the indication for the practice of communication across the socioeconomic, cultural and geographic boundaries separating the two neighborhoods. Community jargon, with its connotations of solidarity and "we-feeling," averts the possibility of stigmatic associations of dependency, charity and a dichotomy between benefactor and beneficiary. It is hardly surprising, therefore, that a significant bulk of the funds is directed towards the reification in the most material manner of the idea of community, that is, the construction of the Matnas building, known as the community center.

The imputed materality of the "partnership" between the two "committees" is described through the eyes of the interviewee mainly in terms of good-will, Zionist commitment and an opportunity to visit Israel, develop personal relationships and enjoy the hospitality of residents. However, such interest lacks the solidity, depth and permanency of a long-lasting bond so needed for the future existence of the project. This is rectified in another local newspaper article based on an interview with a married couple from the sponsoring community:

> The particular story of Mr. and Mrs. J. from B in the Project Renewal Scheme at Arod neighborhood, illlustrates the links that have developed between two very different communities.
>
> When the United Jewish Community of B was offered the chance to be partners with the Arod neighborhood, the family was already involved in Israel. Both Mr. and Mrs. J. are concentration camp survivors who had vowed that if ever they came out of Bergen-Belsen alive, they would create a link and a home in Israel. They build their own house in Herzliya Pituach in 1981-1982.
>
> This dream took many years to fulfill, because after the war ended, rather than face the prospect of being interned in a British army camp in Cyprus if they embarked for Palestine, then blockaded, they left for the United States.
>
> The couple's initial involvement in Jewish communal work in New York was through the Sephardic Jewish Brotherhood Welfare Association. Subsequently, they engaged in voluntary work for the United Jewish Community of B.
>
> This commitment is traceable to their family backgrounds, especially childhood and youth in German Jewish families. Mr. J's maternal grandfather, whom Mr. J. accompanied on visits to Palestine in 1912 and 1928, was a cofounder of the Sha'arei Zedek hospital in Jerusalem.

After graduating from Hamburg University School of Law, Mr. J. was obliged to flee Nazi Germany in 1938, escaping across the Yugoslavian border and into Greece. He found work in Salonika, and when the Nazis occupied Greece in 1941, he and Mrs. J.—born and educated in that country—had been married only three weeks. They were deported with the entire Jewish community to Bergen Belsen, separated during their internment and reunited after the war. Mr. J. lost his family in the concentration camps.

Mrs. J., who has a facility for foreign languages and gift for self-expression, recalls that "I used to have two wishes, I repeated over and over to myself in the camp. I vowed that if I came out alive, I would catch up on all sleepless hours, days and nights and the terrible weariness we experienced. And I promised myself that if reunited with my husband, we would build a home in Eretz Yisrael" [Land of Israel].

The chance to participate in Project Renewal, through a partnership and twinning link with an Israeli neighborhood, was a culmination of many years of seeking an outlet not just for a home in Israel—which they built—but also for direct involvement in serving Israeli rehabilitation programs.

Like those American Jews who support Israel vigorously—partly to recompense for what they were to do during World War II and afterwards—the J's commitment is intended to give new life to individuals and groups who have been victims of deprivation. As Holocaust survivors, they never forgot the brutalities of camp conditions, but nevertheless emphasized in as many ways possible, the hopes and dreams they share for a better future.

Common Jewish heritage does not seem to be sufficient to furnish and safeguard a continuing linkage between the residents of Arod, most of whom are of Afro-Asian extraction, and the originally European, well-to-do Jewish inhabitants of B. Hence the commitment to Israel and particularly to its underprivileged citizens is associated albeit implausibly, to the experience of the Holocaust on the one hand and to the need attributed to American Jewry to seek moral absolution for their alleged indifference to the fate of their European brethren during World War II.

Described as deep-rooted and unconditional, the obligation toward the neighborhood is set in a frame of reference where the destiny of the Jewish people is interwoven into the current problems and signify dissolution of historical, geographical and sociocultural boundaries.

The result of this rhetorical imagery was, among, other things, an invitation published in the Israeli English daily newspaper, *The Jerusalem Post,* where all B residents visiting Israel were called upon to participate in the opening of the new community center. The title of that invitation stated: "The United Jewish Community of B and Project Renewal of Arod (in) PARTNERS FOR LIFE."

The director of the social project spelled out the meaning of this partnership and the contribution of Arod towards its fostering in a paper presented in a forum of community leaders.

> I want to stress the personal element that developed in the meetings over the years between visitors from B and Arod residents. The warmth of these encounters, usually in the private homes of our residents, the hospitality and the response to—were and are outstanding. These regular meetings, I hope and believe, have given our Diaspora Jewish brothers a real sense of partnership and belonging, and a concrete involvement in the rehabilitation of the neighborhood. They have certainly behaved like real partners, and never insisted on our acceptance of their approach to a particular matter, just because they were contributing the funds.

And:

> The involvement in Project Renewal carries with it status in Jewish communal life, and has served as a stepping-stone to the highest communal offices for many lay leaders. There have been cases where peer pressures were a major factor in the involvement of certain individuals, as well as a desire for social recognition. Still, if such motives were instrumental, I can think of few examples where they had such positive and constructive outcomes. At any rate, it is possible to understand Israel-Diaspora relations, as least in one sense, as an *exchange.* The Diaspora gives economic and political support, while Israel returns a variety of social benefits, including the communal status associated with philanthropy, encounters with Israel's political elite, and so on, as well as Jewish identity reinforcement.

Warmth, hospitality, a sense of belonging, identity and status are the rewards described by the director as constituting the part of the neighborhood in the trade-off with the American benefactors. These are assets whose value cannot be equated in monetary terms, and hence, although exchangeable, their uniqueness is preserved and so are the boundaries between the two "communities." As long as these boundaries are maintained both parties can continue to develop their mutual interests. Close personal attachments, therefore, which by their very nature might pose a threat to those established demarcation lines, become undesirable. Thus personal distance must be sustained and a fine balance between "warmth" and "dependency" has to be struck. In the exhorting words of the director:

> Without in any way belittling or underestimating those cases in which long-lasting, personal relationships resulted from Project Renewal, my own sense is that they were exceptional. This has to be said in order to prevent the disappointments which expectations of such personal ties would likely produce. I do think that a very profound dynamic has occurred at the broader level of neighborhood-Diaspora community relations, and this is a reality with major creative potential for the long term. It would be a mistake to insist on its immediate translation into a network of deep personal friendships, which is unlikely to happen. Rather, we should approach this as a process to be nurtured and developed over time.

It is this need to maintain a sense of uniqueness, while endeavoring to exploit this very sense to assimilate into the broader social environment, that also marks the relationship with the municipal milieu of the neighborhood. This dilemma of seeking political integration while maintaining the justification for such a claim, that is, the status of Arod as a definable community, is manifested in almost all the descriptive activity pertaining to the relationship between the town Netanya and the neighborhood.

Under the title "The Slogan: Netanya by Arod's Side is Coming True," the chairman of the residents' executive council writes in the local newspaper:

> The road [to the new community center] has been difficult; beginning with a dilapidated building furnished with rickety chairs, continuing in another building lacking any halo of culture till it had been renovated to become a small, warm home. Thus, in slow steps of a corner here and an air-raid shelter there, we have materialized this idea [of becoming a community] that the Arod community has lovingly accepted and harnessed itself to the activity of changing its image and proving itself as a constructive and contributing community.

Having reified the notion of a positive community, a claim for power sharing in the municipal arena can now be made:

> It is difficult for me to avoid a bit of unpleasant nostalgia. One of the national evening dailies once published an article saying that Arod is the black spot of the town of Netanya. Today I am delighted to say how happy we are that it is to our credit that we can prove that Arod is a shining and blessed spot of Netanya which will, in years to come, influence the actual culture of the society in the entire city.

This descriptive commentary of another descriptive practice leads to yet another description—this time of the inevitable consequence of this changing relationship between Arod and Netanya:

> All the necessary measures have been taken to turn this house [the community center] into a cultural center for the whole town and to create a real and natural integration between the inhabitants of the city and the residents of Arod and among themselves. This house, by the contents infused in it, will be able to generate unmediated meetings between the various populations, something, which in spite of plans and efforts, is not always successfully accomplished. Here, in this place, it will be accomplished by itself and naturally, and will leave its mark on the relationships that will be forged between the residents of the neighborhood and the town.

The apparent contradiction built into this text between the insistence on "integration" and the dichotomy of "we" and "they," "us" and "them," "Arod" and "the town" is resolved by resorting to the fatalistic certainty of "nature" of the mysterious determinism inherent in the nature of things "by itself."

The new community center, being a concrete symbol of Arod's ambivalent role in the municipal arena, serves also in the words of the chairman of the residents council as a generator for almost an apocalyptic vision transcending the problematics of the intricate links between town and neighborhood:

> I am certain that we have a supreme duty at this time to lend a hand and do our best to consolidate the community programs in this center and our objective is to redeem our neighborhood and children with the People of Israel as a whole. May the Jewish New Year bring peace in our region and a time of greater sanctification of values for our people to live in this land

of the Bible, and in the spirit of our ancient prophets let us wish all a Happy New Year and seasons of joyfulness, Amen.

Described though as it was as a dream-come-true, the town politicians expressed apprehension as to the changes in power structure envisioned by Arod's local leadership. The pattern of patronage that characterized previous relationships with the town was not to be abandoned, and although solemn pledges were made by the Mayor and his aids to support the operation of the community center, a strong case was also made for the "self-sufficiency of the center and for the fostering of continuing sponsorship by the American community." As the Mayor stated: "The center is the realization of a dream shared by all those who wished to do Arod good." The hierarchy between a benefactor and a beneficiary is still maintained and possibly reinforced.

Arod's leaders, being well-aware of this unmitigated attitude toward them at the municipal level, set to explore arenas of power and recognition in the statutory level. Hence ample descriptive space was given to visits to the new community center of some prominent national personalities, of which the finance minister's tour of the neighborhood and the building made the headline for the local newspapers' special issue for the opening of the center. A repeated mention was made of the fact that the minister spent a great deal of time and showed keen interest in the center, and that it was presented to him as the showpiece of the town.

The desire to be on equal footing with other, better established, sectors of Israeli society also featured highly in the description of activists taking place in the neighborhood.

II. THE RHETORICS OF PRACTICE

The idea of community is rhetorically processed not only with regard to its descriptive constituents but also through the reflection of its practical manifestations in the printed media. This section, therefore, is set to explore some of the facets of the recording of public activities as advertised and described in local publications. This is to say that activists themselves are excluded from this discussion. It is the depiction of both organized and spontaneous

Table VI.1. Weekly Programs Scheduled by the Matnas

Youth Movement (ages 9-18)
Instructor's Course (14-16)
Enrichment Activities (15-18)
Army Preparation (17-18)
Instructors Meetings
Activities (7-8; 8-9)
Enrichment Activities for Instructors

Youth Club
Social Programs
Movies
Army Preparation
Theater
Parties

Sports
Gymnastics (grouped by Age)
Football (grouped by Age)
Karate (grouped by Age)
Volleyball (boys 10-14)
Ballet (girls 5-7; 8-11)
Skate-Boarding (mixed, ages 6-12)
Body-Building (15+)
Rope-Pulling (15+)
Basketball (9-12; 13-15; Youth and Adults)
Table Tennis
Physical Fitness
Folk Dancing (children; adults)

Library
Lending and Browsing
Special Activities

Adult Education
Morning Studies
Evening Studies
Studies for Elderly Women
English Courses
Adult Education College
High School for Adults

Parenthood
Instructing Instructors
Meeting with Parents
Home Visits

Studies Center
English Lessons with Computers (grades 6-7)
Mathematics with Computers (grades 7-8)
Enrichment/Social Activities (grades 7-8)
English, Mathematics, Physics (high school)

Old Age Clubs
Handicrafts
Literacy Courses
Jewish Studies
Keeping Fit
General Activities (story-telling, dancing, outings, etc.)

148

Cultural Events
Coffee Mornings
Local Theater
Geography of Israel

Motherhood
Instructors' Meetings
Mothers' Meetings
Mothers' and Children's Meetings

Welfare Activities—Reception Hours
Chief Social Worker
Occupational Counselling
Psychologist
Social Worker's Assessments
Family and Child Welfare Worker
Children's Welfare Counselors
Elementary School Welfare Workers
Girls' Welfare Worker
Social Worker for the Aged
Care-Attendants for the Aged
Young Adults' Welfare Worker
Employment Coordinator
Eligibility Counselor

Children's Welfare
Long-Day Kindergarten
Game Center
Children's Club
Girls' Club

Religious Culture
Jewish Law
Talmud Lessons
Judaism for Women
The Weekly Portion
Jewish Philosophy
Bar-Mitzvah Preparatory Course

community activities with which our analysis is concerned. Here again, we witness the delineation of boundaries vis-à-vis systems of accountability.

Distributed in the neighborhood and disseminated among officials and offices concerned with Project Renewal, the following chart of weekly programs annually scheduled to take place within the setting of the Matnas attests to an aspired image of action-centered community (see Table VI.1). All the activities advertised are meticulously timetabled and properly sited. The first name of the organizer or of the person in charge is also printed to infuse the very formal form of presentation with informal familiarity.

Life in the neighborhood is depicted as being channeled through a web of organized programs of activity with only a few areas of existence spared. As indicated before (Chapter II), with social differentiation being abandoned to the idea of community, age and sex became the principal organizing factors for allocating activities and forming group divisions.

The all-embracing totality of this community blueprint is underlined by a few assumptions regarding the social profile of Arod residents. A great number of the offered programs are designed to cater for the socialization of residents to roles to be assumed by them in the near future. Thus preparatory courses for military service, ancillary educational projects and efficient motherhood training, while providing support for specific encounters, also suggest some mistrust in the potential ability of residents to successfully accomplish such social undertakings. So salient is the diffident approach towards residents' capabilities that almost nothing is left to spontaneity and grass-root initiative. Even those in charge of nurturing the residents are expected to cultivate and "enrich" their own resources through meetings and courses included in the overall scheme.

This assumption of having residents "in need of fostering" is incongruous with the image of an independent, destigmatized community that the scheme projects. It is this contradiction between a patronizing structure and a self-help association that makes for the juxtaposition of modernity-oriented ventures, such as computer-based courses and literacy classes, on the one hand, and welfare activities, on the other. The aspect of self-reliance and autonomy is punctuated in a number of "community events" described in the local newspaper: a successful appeal to the public to collect donations for the funding of an open-heart surgery abroad to save the life of a little girl; elderly caring for the elderly; finding a suitable place to celebrate a Bar-Mitzvah ceremony; the setting up of informal groups for playing music, and so on—all attesting to the indispensibility of the community in providing a sense of identity, real care and in being the last resort for emergencies concerning situational predicaments or life-crises. The obituaries as well as the congratulatory notices published in the paper endows the work of community-building with a personal-familial dimension and depicts the neighborhood as a "life-term arena" with its own rewards, status symbols and codes of practice.

The assumption that the activities in Arod community are under way legitimizes claims for belonging to and identifying with the broader spectrum of Israeli culture, thereby expanding boundaries and systems of accountability. These newly encroached upon territories are described in terms of arenas of activities now open to residents.

Hence, two pages in one issue of the local newspaper contain articles describing the involvement of the border-police in the neighborhood, the activities of the local branch of the home-guard, the setting up of a citizens advice bureau, the local club of one of the national sports organizations and the nature of a talmudic debate pertaining to the restricted agricultural cultivation of the land in certain years. The Arod community is thus described as part and parcel of its sociocultural milieu. This culminates in the wide publicity that was given to the annual pilgrimage of the novices of the local youth-movement to Massada—a prominent symbol of the Israeli national myth and ethos representing an unconditional martyrial commitment to the faith. This, alongside a call for residents to join a trip to Jersualem and to witness the ceremonial award of the "Crown of Torah" by the chief Rabbi to the prime minister, predicates the legitimacy of the community on its Israeli and Jewish identity.

Having been culturally chartered, the neighborhood can pronounce its claims for power-sharing in the municipal arena. These claims are also phrased in terms of activities, particularly those held in the new building of the Matnas. Thus, Arod "invites" inhabitants of Netanya to take part in the bustling activities of the cultural center and to enjoy the facilities, some of which—computers, for example—are in the vanguard of development in Netanya.

In return, the municipality also "invites" Arod residents to take a stroll along the newly developed sidewalk and to raise their problems and queries in an open meeting with the mayor. Described as a hybrid between guest and burgess, the residents of Arod find themselves in a bargaining situation where the symbolic center of their community can be exchanged for and abandoned to a more central place in the political life of the town.

A solution to this predicament is offered in an article describing the building as "a home" for the residents while emphasizing that the internal design of the premises is flexible enough to accommodate an infinite variety of activities and to cater for a multitude of possible needs. This is to say that even though the Matnas is the home of Arod's residents, its utilization is open to negotiation. Stressing that the auditorium attached to the main building is of the most modern design and is modeled on the better-equipped entertainment halls in the country, the article implies that this particular facility can serve a much wider population than that of Arod. The following section describes how this dual message is ceremonially transmitted in the course of the inaugural activities surrounding the opening of the community center.

As we shall see, the assumptions guiding the rhetorics of community are not necessarily reflected in the social reality in Arod. This should be reiterated at this stage, because the notion of ceremony or ritual—be it "religious" or "secular"—might suggest otherwise.

III.   CEREMONIAL RHETORIC

The descriptive celebration of the idea of community reached its symbolic climax in the inaugural ceremony of the new community center. Being a condensed and indivisible form of rhetorical media, the ceremony employed a fusion of audio-visual means to reflect, reinforce and generate manifestations of accountability and boundaries. The community was thus presented and represented in its purest ideal form, with the undesirable slugs of social problems, local conflicts and discontented residents expurgated from the displayed text and its agenda. The neighborhood context became contradictory to the ceremonial context and the split between the two, as discussed in the second chapter of this book, was yet again thrown into relief.

It should be noted at the outset of this section that it is no coincidence that the analytic framework of ritual is not invoked to decipher the social properties of the public event under study. It is not the pursuit and elucidation of a symbolic structure of meanings that guides our analysis. Rather, it is the assumption that the ceremony lends itself to be interpreted as an autonomous system of speech acts, visual displays and reported atmosphere. Analytically, therefore, we refrain from employing the conceptual scope of "ritual" and prefer to premise the discussion on the social world perspective that renders the object of activity—in our case the notion of community—viable in its own right.

Contrary to the turgid, flowery local newspapers' reports on the ceremony, some of which were embroidered with biblical verses and phrased as myths or fairy tales, the residents' reaction to the event was muted. Not only was grandiose language absent from their references to the opening, but many of them were completely unaware of and uninterested in the much publicized occurrence. Thus, while arriving at the neighborhood, some of the invited guests happened to ask a group of residents basking in the afternoon sun for directions to the site of the center. Having had to repeat their inquiry a few times, one of the residents retorted: "No idea what you are talking about."

Indeed, only a few residents received invitations to the event, most of them either in the official capacity as local committee members or as live exhibits of ethnic folklore. Only holders of invitations were allowed entry into the fenced grounds of the community center. Telling of this separation between residents and the symbol of their community was the invitation itself. Designed as a wedding invitation, the folded glossy stiff paper, illustrated with an artist's impression of the center and carrying the various emblems of the public organs involved was bilingually phrased and presented as follows:

The Jewish Agency of Israel
Renewal Department
United Jewish Appeal

Municipality of Netanya

Residents of Arod and the
United Jewish Community of "B"
"Partners—Now & Forever"

Request the honor of your presence
on Thursday, October 23rd, 1986, at 4 p.m.
for the Dedication of
the Community Center, Arod, Netanya

Program:
   4:00 p.m.: *Reception of "B" Mission.*
   4:30 p.m.: *Opening Ceremonies & Tour of the Building*
   8:00 p.m.: *Performance in the New Auditorium:*
                Netanya Orchestra
                Greetings
                Dance Group
                Arod—an Audio Visual Presentation
                Choir and Dance Troupes

Before proceeding to analyze the text of the English version, a mention must be made of some noted differences between that and the Hebrew counterfoil. Designated to appeal to the Israeli guests, the invitation contained precise directions as to the location of the event and more specified details of the program. Also the name of the compère, a famous radio and T.V. personality, which was omitted from the English version, was boldly printed. This attempt to extend the boundaries of the Matnas to the national arena by addressing core images of Israeli culture was made through the Hebrew reterming of the building. Whereas the Matnas had been turned into "a community center" to account for the common ground with the American counterpart, the Hebrew version coined it, "the temple of culture"—a title invoking desirable associations of the Tel Aviv main concert hall, the house of the Israeli philharmonic orchestra, which is also called "the temple of culture."

While the Jewish Agency and the municipality of Netanya are allocated separate spaces, the sponsor and the sponsored are merged in a descriptive bond of eternal fraternity as "Partners— now—and forever." Indicative though as it is of the joint enterprise of building the community center, the main message embedded in the invitation was in the relations between the participants. The Jewish Agency and the municipality were placed on equal footing with the partnership between the two communities. Thus, the strength and potency of Arod to negotiate terms with either the Jewish Agency or the municipality was graphically and verbally depicted as a product of the marriage between Arod and B. Subsequently, the generous inclusion of Netanya in the program (the mayor, the town orchestra, the emblem) was descriptively contingent upon the inextricable association between the two partners. The boundaries of accountability were thus redelineated and reified. The following description attests to this claim.

On the day of the event, the American mission, having been wined and dined at a Tel Aviv hotel, was transported by coach to the neighborhood, where very few residents, most of them passers-by, welcomed them. However, a well organized reception party composed of local dignitaries and the military-like attired regiments of Arod's youth movement awaited them anxiously. Waving Israeli and neighborhood banners, singing, chanting and distributing bunches of flowers to the guests, the children mingled with the visitors to form a disorderly procession leisurely heading toward the site of the community center. At the gates the mission was ushered in while the children and the accompanying residents were barred from the premises. With no protest, the residents stayed outside and watched the outdoor part of the ceremony held at the front patio of the building.

From far north in the Galilee a Rabbi who acquired a nationwide reputation as a successful rehabilitator of convicts was brought to affix the Mezuzzot on the main doorway and on the doorposts inside the building. It is important to note that although the majority of residents are of Eastern origin, the Rabbi chosen to carry out this religious act was of Ashkenazi extraction and a well known figure in the Israeli ecclesiastical establishment. It was the combination of the two facts—social fame in rehabilitation and his religious standing—that made for electing for this task a Rabbi whose verse of prayer was alien to most of Arod's residents. The elimination of the ethnic element was to become a recurrent theme through the ensuing ceremony.

Having jointly hoisted the banner of B, unveiled the dedication plaque and cut the ribbon, the mayor of Netanya and the dignitaries of B entered the building accompanied by Jewish Agency officials and the local staff of the Matnas. Inside they found a table laden with civil guard and traffic-police leaflets, a group of dancing women adorned with ethnic costumes and matching jewelry and children sitting in the library poised with open books to welcome "the important guests."

The Rabbi dedicated the various rooms and halls to the names of the donors who, in turn, danced with Torah scrolls and joined the Rabbi in chanting verses taken from the customary Jewish wedding ceremony to indicate the completion of the ritual of matrimonial wedlock. In between these acts, music playing and dancing took place with the guests joining hands with the ethnically dressed women in a circle of Israeli folk dances. This part of the event ended with the guests being dispersed to residents' homes for supper. They reassembled at 8 o'clock in the evening at the auditorium to attend the rest of the program. Suitably attired for the occasion, the invited audience filled up the lavishly decorated hall to await what was described later in the local paper as "the house-warming of the temple." While the American delegation crowded the front rows, the very few residents invited took their seats at the back distancing themselves from the occurrence by directing their looks sideways rather than forward, searching for familiar faces and exchanging snide remarks such as "It turns out that we are really the visitors here."

The subsequent show corroborated and reinforced that sense of alienation and nonbelonging to the atmosphere of the ceremony. Starting with a musical prelude by the town orchestra of Netanya, which played a chain of well-known Israeli tunes followed by songs from "Fiddler on the Roof," the show continued in a parade of dignitaries addressing the audience with speeches fit for the occasion.

Seated on stage to face the audience, the group of speakers reflected the extended boundaries of the neighborhood. Next to each other and in no order of importance were sitting the mayor of Netanya, the director of the social project, the president of the residents' committee, a few representatives of the American community and a minister in the Israeli cabinet. After introductory hand-shaking, the compère called on the speakers to address the audience, with each speech delivered in both English and Hebrew. In fact, the gestures made by the speakers, coupled with the content of their texts, suggested that the target for the messages conveyed on stage was a reflexive one, meaning, the speakers themselves.

Thus, the mayor of Netanya was self-congratulatory by emphasizing the role his municipality played in developing the ties with the American community, hence forfeiting the sole privilege of Arod's leadership in cultivating the relationship. The president of the residents' committee hailed the endeavors and spirit of the community, while the director—a resident himself— exaulted the joint accomplishments of the two communities. The American delegates in turn articulated the view that Arod has offered them "a second home" and "a feeling of belonging to a warm, loving family." The minister, while talking about the national significance of Project Renewal and the example that Arod set for other communities, stressed the initiative taken by the Likud government of Menachem Begin in embarking on the course of rehabilitation and implementing it through its politices.

While the political allusion elicited very little response from the audience, the emotionality laden locutions such as "family," "love" and "unison" won unequivocal applause. So did the gesture made to two of the American sponsors who were presented with engraved brass trophies endorsed by the prime minister of Israel in recognition of their contribution to the country and to the Jewish people. This was received by the audience with a standing ovation.

The audio-visual show that followed furnished the notion of Arod's place in the broad universe of the town, the state, world Jewry, and indeed, within the value system of Western society. Local dancers performed jazz and cancan styles; the Arod grammar-school choir sang American folk songs in English and a couple of well-known Israeli singers urged the apathetic audience to join in a sing-along of Hassidic and popular Israeli songs. The ethnic element was evident in its absence and so was any mention of the plight of "second Israel." If this message of integration with the "first Israel" was not clear enough, the two singers accompanied their musical performance with a slide show in which, side by side on the one screen, pairs of pictures were simultaneously projected; one depicting familiar Israeli scenes (Jerusalem, the sea of Galilee, the Negev) and the other showing happy moments in Arod's renewed life (improved houses, public places, smiling residents and sponsors' visits). The evening ended with the members of the local youth movement entering the stage, waving banners and singing "we brought peace upon you"—a song familiar to Israelis. By that time (around 12 o'clock at night) the auditorium was vacated by all the residents and by most of the American guests.

It is the gulf between the notion of community and the actual neighborhood that the rhetorics of community developed in Arod come to preserve. The town, the nation, the state and the Jewish people are juxtaposed and mixed in a self-contained, self-fulfilling rhetorical universe. In contrast, the self-effacing residents, whose part in the construction of that notion is constantly and consistently denied, are placed outside the scope of that universe. The opportunity to extend the boundaries of the community, therefore, is contingent upon the obliteration of the neighborhood as a viable social entity. In that sense the former and the latter become mutually exclusive. The reflexivity of the rhetorical act and its embedment in descriptive activities rather than in action, make for a situation where deeds do not necessarily inform words and images.

This separation, which is grounded in practical considerations and functional contexts, furnishes the social world perspective with a further dimension. The social world of community is not only divorced from what its core object, community as an existing social unit, purports to represent, but is also the reverse mirror image of that object. For the idea of community to gather momentum, generate novel channels of communication and acquire new contents, the former basis for its inception has to be relinquished and sometimes even negated. Thus boundaries and systems of accountability can only proliferate to the advantage of those involved in the rhetorics of community, if they are not aborted by the deficiencies of the social constraints from which they emerge.

This last point of the necessary discrepancy between the viability of the social world of community and the social context of the community suggests an intriguing split between meaning, that is, the social world, and symbol, the actual community—a split that accounts for some of the independent characteristics of the rhetorics of community. The following incident demonstrates both the incongruity and the interlinkage between the two.

On the day the cornerstone for Arod's community center was laid, a bus of sponsors from the American community arrived at the site. While the guests took part in the ceremony of founding a community for Arod, the bus was broken into and money and valuables were stolen from it. It took the project staff a whole night to find the culprits—local youths—and return the stolen items to their benefactors. Embarrassed as they were, both parties to the enterprise pronounced that the occurrence would only strengthen their conviction in the importance of community creation for the residents.

Chapter VII

Community:
Phenomenon into Concept

The purpose of this chapter is neither to conclude nor to sum up. Too many open questions and unfinished issues forestall any meaningful attempt to embark on such a discourse. Instead, an analytic cycle will be closed by reverting the relations between community as a concept and community as a phenomenon to the original form presented at the outset of our discussion, that is, phenomenon into concept. We began by asserting that the sociological properties of the concept are ill-informed by the corollaries of the social phenomenon and suggested that through the application of the construct of social world, an approach could be formulated to handle the former as a manifestation of the latter. Now, having examined some of the characteristics of community as a social phenomenon, it seems apropriate to elicit from research findings a few observations concerning the conceptual profile of community.

This will be pursued by considering three issues, each elucidating one aspect of the social world of community vis-à-vis its analytic implications. It is hoped that by providing some theoretical underpinnings to the discussion, it will offer a comparative framework for addressing similar phenomena in different settings and contexts.

The first section of the discussion revisits the four dimensions of the concept of community through their respective existential dilemmas. The second section ascertains the coordinates of the process of transforming sentiment into structure within the framework of the social world of community, while the third section sets out to explore some of the sociological properties of that social world. Following some of our preliminary suggestions (see Chapter I, section II), it is argued that the social world perspective offers an expedient analytic tool for the study of modern settings in terms of their symbolic and interactional organizations. This leads to reflections on what seems to me to be a significant contribution of this approach to the sociological and anthropological preoccupation with the nature of symbolic forms and symbolic action.

I. COMMUNITY REVISITED

The mushrooming of community as a social world described in the ethnography stands in inverse relation to the "eclipse of community" (Stein 1972) as a form of social organization. Our findings do not support Redfield's definition of a "little community" (Redfield 1955) as a homogeneous self-conscious social unit, nor do they conform to territorially-based divisions (Poplin 1979),[1] nor to characteristics of intensive interaction (Bell and Newby 1971; Webber 1964). Even the broad and dynamic view expounded by Martindale (1964) of a community as a social devise made of "a set or system of groups sufficient to solve all the basic problems of ordinary ways of life" (p. 64) does not seem to befit the disparity of resources and the range of alternative, sometimes competing, "solutions" found in Arod. Yet in the absence of community structure, an apparent community symbolism thrives. Moreover, from a nebulous obscurity the theme of "community" evolves to acquire distinct social properties whose manifestations can be scanned in the domains of boundaries, culture, function and time. The introduction of community into these four existential spheres induce tensions, but also offer solutions, the essence of which is the subject of the following discussion.

Rather than "maintaining" one set of boundaries—territorial, residential, welfare-oriented, bureaucratically defined—the social world of community generates rules of delineation and provides corresponding markers to stamp them.

The maps of community sketched out in Arod are drawn within coordinates of accountability to various other social worlds or to different subworlds of community. Thus, the welfare workers, whose professional commitment and interests dictate a problem-laden futuristic image of community, interweave their career aspirations and biographical trajectories into the fabric of Arod's reality to produce their own version of community. Likewise, but in a different vein of accountability, project workers adhere to an atemporal diffuse ethos of depersonalized community in pursuit of their interests and in accordance with their social condition.

The set of negotiable qualities of community, which are discovered and exploited by residents, is cast into an area of overlapping circles of conceptions of community in the hope of yielding positive gains. Within that area of coincidental agreement, community is shared by all participants as grounds for negotiating cultural identities and distributing power and temporal orientation. Outside those common boundaries, the ambition of community preoccupation is shifted to other social worlds, such as welfare management or municipal politics, or else to other subworlds of community, like those appealing to the American counterparts of the neighborhood. In either case, ideological doctrines, cultural idioms and vested interests are channeled towards and from the appropriate systems of accountability wherein the participant is anchored.

The first issue to be negotiated within the framework of the social world of community is the dilemma of cultural identity. Here "community" offers an alternative category of identification to the deeply entrenched social criteria of classification in Israeli society, ethnicity, deprivation, political allegiance and mode of life (kibbutz, moshav, urban setting). The social option of a community-bound definition contains a promise of a stigma-free identity and a new start for the stereotype-laden residents. However, the encroachment of those very stereotypes and their concomitant social worlds thwarts any practical realization of such alternative. Community is neither a cultural vacuum, nor an omnipotent social leverage. Rather, it proves to be a cultural strategy defeating its own object.

The self-subversiveness of the strategy of using community to attain social goals is extended to the political arena of mobilizing resources. The promise of "urban renewal" turns the sponsorship of the project into a trap of dependency, with "community" providing the rationale and the legitimacy for perpetuating it. The ritualistic function of community, in bestowing an image of autonomy on a highly dependent social milieu, cannot be overrated. On the other hand, the amorphous nature of the basis of that social world enables elective participation and elusive commitment, so that action does not have to follow apparent conviction and practice is divorced from symbol.

The temporal dimension of community encapsulates and epitomizes all the preceding issues. Being at the heart of their everyday experience, the paradox of immutable change and of terminal continuity infuses the residents' community-centered social world with irreconcilable temporal incongruity. The multilevel time universe of "community," as reinforced by the structural constraints embedded in the operation of the project, distinguishes that social world from other realities. Hence it was rendered unique, both as a social world and as a piece in the mosaic of other sponsored urban-renewal schemes. Here the much discussed "urban life experience"[2] does not lend itself to sweeping generalizations, for neither in construction nor in content can the social world of community developed in Arod be likened to other superficially similar settings.

Nonetheless, the forms and modes underpinning the constitution of that social world are amenable to extrapolation to structurally comparable phenomena. It is at this point that some general characteristics of the social world at hand call for further elucidation.

II. SENTIMENT INTO STRUCTURE

The overlapping area of shared communication is neither arbitrarily "taken for granted," nor socially "given" to the participants. Rather, having the uncertainty and ambiguity of novelty as its breeding ground, the core of the social world of community in Arod develops through a process transforming vague commonalities into a social area of action; or, to put it within a broader frame of reference, from sentiment into structure.

Although chronologically uncharted,[3] this transformation can be analyzed as a social process, albeit not in terms of time sequences, but as the dynamics of interlocking social factors. Gripped by dilemmas, vicious circles and backlashes, the analysis of the evolution of community as a social world through the prism of sentiment into structure is a far cry from an orderly linear progression of causally linked events.

Unlike culturally established objects, such as the art and collector's items, or social phenomena, such as alcoholism and aging (see Chapter I, section III, for discussion of the social world), community has neither communicative value nor institutionalized conveyance procedures. These have to be negotiated and formulated in the course of everyday interactions. Guided by economic and political interests and molded by newly-acquired cultural idioms, the concept of community takes shapes and forms of social transactions whose existence as "facts" in their own right is the cornerstone for that transformation. That communication is inseparable from interaction (Heilman 1979) and, therefore, the social world of community, or any social world for that matter is a transactional set, is almost self-evident.[4] However, the argument that the dynamics of those interactions are fueled and sustained by contradiction and dilemmas needs further elucidation.

The emergent structure of community-bound interactions is neither consistent nor congruous. Yet it is invested with enough social properties to make it into a viable arena of action geared toward goals and consisting of negotiations governed by rational interests. Paradoxical as it is, the social world of community offers means toward ends and renders the desirable attainable. To understand that apparent contradiction between the "rationality" of the structure and the paradoxality of its underpinnings, it is necessary to ponder the validity of the question rather than to fathom the possible answers. For example, if the social activities concerning community in Arod can be identified as "rituals" or "myths," readily available anthropological interpretation of resolving contradictions might be broached. However, as is argued in the next section, "community" is neither a social ritual nor a cultural narrative. Hence such interpretations obscure, rather than illuminate, the issue.

Our approach follows a multitude of studies (see, for example, Augé 1982; Bateson 1966; Murphy 1971, 1977),[5] whose focus on contradiction and paradox attests to its centrality in human behavior.[6] Or, to quote Moore (1975, p. 234):

> The assumption is that it is useful to conceive an underlying, theoretically absolute cultural and social indeterminancy which is only partially done away with by culture and organized social life, the patterned aspects of which are temporary, incomplete and contain elements of inconsistency, ambiguity, discontinuity, contradiction, paradox and conflict. The issue, therefore, at stake is not why there are such incongruities, but how they shape and manipulate social life.

It has already been suggested (see Chapter V, section IV) that the community-bound dilemmas enmesh participants in a web of constraints, which in turn, reinforce, reproduce and perpetuate the social condition from which they stem. This process has been previously shown to be a delineator of social boundaries, not through internal or external definitions as suggested by Ross (1975), but via the operation of the emergent properties of the social world of community. It is precisely this process that is responsible for the transformation of sentiment into structure.

If the dilemmas inherent in the social world of community are to be considered as the main variables in the patterning of social transaction, which in turn, can be formulated in terms of a social structure, then Barth's (1966) generative model of process and form seems to lend itself to serve as a conceptual framework for that transformation. As Barth (1966) suggests, various permutations of variables produce different social forms, meaning, social structures and selected model combinations of those variables ought to be compared to available observable realities.

It is our contention that given the existence and impact of the four dilemmas, their manifestations in terms of social form may alter with changing contexts, situations and participants. Thus, our interpretation of Arod's community-imbued social world can be applied to other realities composed of similar social components. The specificity of each such interpretation, however, is conferred on a certain context under study both by the differences in substance and by variegated patterns of relations between variables. The dynamics of a social world, therefore, are in continuous dialectics between the transactional opportunities embedded in it and constraints and regularized behaviors engendered by it. It is at this point of touching upon the social world perspective as a sociological paradigm that further discussion pertaining to such properties is necessary.

III. COMMUNITY AS A SOCIAL WORLD

The previously mentioned observation (see section I of this chapter) concerning the inverse relationship between the decline of community and the rise of community as a social world can be employed as a point of departure for the following. Notwithstanding the conviction—not the fact, because it is unfalsifiable—that the ideal type of community as a social unit cannot be matched by reality, vestiges of the concept are still prominent in describing and analyzing human groups. The so-called "we-feeling" and the territorial imperative are deemed to be inherent characteristics of many social settings under the guise of community (see Chapter I, section I).

However, as our case study demonstrates, the less *Gemeinschaft*-like "objective" criteria of community are identifiable in a setting, the more blatant and extensive the use of community is. In effect, it can be stated that within the vacuum of community as a social entity, a social world of community orientations has evolved.

The explanation for this intriguing contradiction rests with the nature of a social world—any social world—as product of complex society with its attendant attributes of simplex relationships, compartmentalized structure and diverse symbolic orders. Hence, almost by definition, when community disappears, social worlds are likely to emerge. "Community"-based social worlds are no exception, and they merely stand to corroborate the well-established inconsistency between cultural idioms and social actions. The appeal in our case of "community" as a cultural code and ideological ethos stems from reasons connected with the peculiar social context at hand (see Chapter I, section IV), rather than from an obscure halo effect of a cultural "residual."

It is precisely at that junction of the social and the cultural that social worlds are formed. But unlike other sociocultural entities, such as rituals and roles, social worlds are not nourished by the fusion of social systems and cultural codes, for they are bred and thrive on the ruins of them both. It is not when culture ceases to inform society or vice versa, such as it is in the case of kinship terminology being divorced from actual kin[7] relationships, that social worlds fill the gap. Rather, it is when both the perceived organization of social life and the cultural edifice of one's identity are in disarray that social worlds are constituted. Hence, the emergence of the social world of community in Arod followed an attempt by Project Renewal to demolish social structures and cultural codes that previously, to a certain extent informed each other.

A social world is crystallized around either a culturally endorsed or incipient unit of reference that is separated, isolated and exclusively handled. The emergent social form around which a social world is built is also not necessarily contingent on other social structures, nor is it a product of any such set of roles and norms. It is the loosening and the fragmenting of social control, coupled with the equivocation and suffusion of symbolic orders, that facilitate the interweaving of motley elements into the fabric of a social world.

This social creation assumes some intriguing sociological properties. It is culturally and socially boundless because it transcends recognized boundaries of territorially-confined societies and cultures; yet it can be almost idiosyncratic. It sustains organized interaction without the rules and structure of a formal organization. It requires flexible commitment, but has the potential possessiveness of a self-perpetuating habit. It lacks the standardized configuration of a role, but is rife with expectations. It involves only a part of the "self," yet it can consume the whole personality. It has the potency of a ritual,[8] but is neither transformatory (see Moore and Myerhoff 1977, p. 13)[9] nor symbolic.

This last issue of the symbolic qualities or their absence from the idea of the social world seems to me to be the most crucial and distinctive feature of that perspective. However wide, almost infinite, the scholarly scope of addressing concepts of symbol and symbolism is, there is one underlying uniting theme that lays a common denominator to all approaches and perspectives on the subject. This is the assumption that any symbol must imply a relation between a signifier (the symbol—the sign—the signal) and a signified (meaning—signification—referential scope) (see Leach 1976, p. 12; Skorupski 1976; Augé 1982; Geertz 1973). This anthropological-sociological postulate, implicit or explicit as it may be, regards behavior as a causal consequence of a given sociocultural context wherein materials for creating meanings are available to be selectively infused into symbols and fit into existing symbolic orders.

This view, which is tied to preconceptions of social and cultural boundaries, does not befit the observations made on the social world of community and the suggestions regarding the properties of the social world in general. The significations or meanings of community are constantly generated by the dynamics of the social world and are not simply borrowed, fostered or logically derived from the cultural context in question. In fact, it can be argued that in no point of the research could any of the data be construed as the "meaning" or "perceived meaning" of "community," not even situationally and temporarily.

The area of signification or the referential scope of community is not in the realm of constructing fixed or transitory meanings, but in engendering a pool of transactional potentialities with which and through which the business of existing in an uncertain, unpredictable and incomprehensible world can be pursued. The social world of community, not in spite but possibly because of its "meaninglessness," provides tools to negotiate terms of social survival in an inexorable environment. As such, it pervades the total lives of the participants—ecologically, culturally, function- ally and temporally—and in that respect imbues their reality with a sense of community after all.

This bond is based neither on solidarity in the form of "we- feeling," nor on a network of social control. Rather, it was made possible by a shared system of communiation, which devoid as it is of fixed messages or enduring relationships, provides a new way of expressing interests and justifying interaction. In a word, it is a social world evolving from community sentiment into a social structure whose qualities as a community are quite alien to the conventional image of such an entity.

NOTES

1. Explicit in early research (Lynd and Lynd 1937; Warner and Lunt 1941) the idea of territorial boundaries forming the contours of community is mutely manifested in later studies under the guise of "street corners" (Whyte 1955; Liebow 1967), housing estates and even single room occupancies tied up together by virtue of their common quality of an "unseen community" (Bohannan 1981).

2. The following are but a few examples of the myriad of research into the experience of urban life: Gans (1962), Street et al. (1967), Gans (1972), Greer (1972), Berry (1973), Fischer (1978), Karp, Stone and Yoels (1977). Of particular interest to our analysis is Strauss' (1961) analysis of urban images.

3. For a chronological account of some landmarks in the operation of Project Renewal until the beginning of the study see Ben-Elia (1982).

4. Nonreactive forms of communication (such as certain hobbies, radio listening, television watching, reading, and so forth) must be regarded in the context as modes of interaction, notwithstanding some obvious reservations.

5. The invocation of the structuralist school, and particularly the work of Lévi-Strauss, seems to serve this argument. However, without subscribing to the basic axioms of that intellectual tradition, it should be deemed pointless to draw on their propositions.

6. For a psychosociological approach to the problem of inconsistencies within the self, see Gergen (1968).

7. See, for example, Schneider's (1968) discussion of American kinship or the ethnographic account of putative kinship in Liebow (1967).

8. Although some of the properties of social world are reminiscent attributes ascribed to ritual, particularly in its secular form (see Moore and Myerhoff 1977, p. 16), the overall nature of ritual seems to contradict the very essence of a social world. Apart from the lack of fusion between subject and symbol, just as social worlds, by definition, are devoid of the rigidity that eventually ossifies a ritual form, so is the element of performance and regularity (Tambiah 1979).

9. It should be noted, however, that the study of social world is still young and longitudinal follow-up research might suggest transformation in sociological form over time.

Chapter VIII

Conclusion

Having relinquished the possibility of a search for the meaning of community, the marriage between the social-world perspective and the understanding of "community" calls for some post factum justifications. At this point of conclusion it should be clear that this work has not focused on the question of "what" people mean by "community" but, to use Geertz's (1979) locution, "what they are up to" when "community" is used by them. It is this inquiry that prompts and frames the employment of the social world to come to grips with the complexity of interests, interactions, constraints and opportunities involved in the business of generating a "community."

Presented as a conceptual vehicle through which *etic* constructs are transformed into *emic* phenomena and vice versa, the concept of social world straddles the social and the sociological. Replete as it is with a multitude of implicit theoretical assumptions, it alludes to many schools of thought, but subscribes to none. Particularly prominent are phenomenological cues that weigh heavily on the underpinnings of the perspective. However, as a deeper scrutiny of the matter is beyond the scope of this discussion, and a short shrift to such epistemological substance should be avoided, suffice it to say that the host of partial commitments to a variety of theoretical stances reflects the basic analytic merit of the social world as a heuristic device.

If, as Fabian (1983) suggests, rapprochement ought to be established between conceptual frameworks and the ethnographic object of inquiry, the social-world approach is answerable in terms

171

of its fragmentary structure, labile boundaries and temporal properties to the profile of social settings it sets to study. This fit is a necessary, albeit not sufficient, condition for any application of a sociological reasoning to the investigation of any given social milieu. The case of community hopefully provided a glimpse into both the usefulness and the problematics of such a quest.

The social world of community is neither a social unit for it lacks boundaries, nor is it a network or a "field" (see Marx 1980), for it does not consider the "self" as its object. Like all other social worlds, its core is not contingent upon interaction or action and hence, its sociological nature escapes the somewhat fruitless discussion concerning the "openness" or "closedness" of social systems. Emerging between the multitude of the institutionalized networks of communication in modern society, social worlds constitute a niche for nascent interests and a scope for forming and developing new contacts without binding commitments. In short, it offers the opportunity to become the search for meanings within an ever changing structure whose dynamics and liability prevent it from ever being accomplished. It is this existential dimension of the social world that is commensurable with some of the major issues associated with modern living, and it is at this point that the implication of the discussion must be left to the reader's consideration.

Another issue that stems from these implications and might warrant the reader's attention is the meaning of social intervention in the light of the emergence of the community-bound social world. It is not oversight or disregard of the abundant literature on the matter that accords such a paucity of consideration to such social substance; rather it was the conviction that addressing the issue in terms of prejudgmental conception of "citizen's participation" and "grass-root involvement" neither benefits the analysis nor reflects the nature of the social reality hitherto recorded. If the consequences of the declared intervention by Project Renewal are to be contemplated in terms of the production of the social world in question, the interpretation of that process might suggest a different vein of understanding it than the conventional way of viewing such matters.

Without discounting the significance and impact of social planning, the findings attest to neither directed changes on a grand scale, nor to the onset of the intended process of cultural revitalization. What has been detected, however, is the incipience of a new opportunity for social negotiation and grappling with existential dilemmas, an opportunity that was created and sustained by the introduction of novel channels of communication into a complex setting. The development and constitution of that emergent property of communication is as unpredictable and uncontrollable as the complexity of the social factors generating it. Hence, the very idea of successful or unsuccessful social intervention is rendered untenable. The dynamics of a social world revolve around the manipulation of a cultural item, rather than around the premediated administration of social control. In that respect, the evolution of sentiment into structure is informed by "grass-root" interests as furnished by available resources and is not a direct manifestation of decisions and policies pertinent to that domain.

Bibliography

Abrams, P. and A. McCulloch. 1976. *Communes, Sociology and Society*. Cambridge: Cambridge University Press.

Arensberg, C. 1955. "American Communities." *American Anthropologist* 57:1143-1162.

Augé, M. 1982. *The Anthropological Circle: Symbol, Function, History*. Cambridge: Cambridge University Press.

Barth, F. 1966. *Models of Social Organization* (Occasional Paper No. 23). London: Royal Anthropological Institute.

————, ed. 1969. *Ethnic Groups and Boundaries*. Boston: Little, Brown.

Barthes, R. 1977. *Image, Music, Text*. London: Fontana.

Bateson, G. 1966. "Information, Codification and Metacommunication." Pp. 412-426 in *Communication and Culture*, edited by A.G. Smith. New York: Holt, Rinehart & Winston.

Becker, H. 1982. *Art Worlds*. Berkeley, CA: University of California Press.

Bell, C. and H. Newby. 1971. *Community Studies*. London: Allen & Unwin.

Ben-Elia, N. 1982. *A Chronology of Key Events in Project Renewal*. Jerusalem: The International Committee for the Evaluation of Project Renewal.

Berkowitz, B. 1984. *Community Dreams*. San Luis Obispo, CA: Impact.

Berry, B.S.L. 1973. *The Human Consequences of Urbanization*. London: Macmillan.

175

Bohannan, P. 1981. "Food of Old People in Centre-City Hotels." Pp. 185-200 in *Dimensions: Aging, Culture and Health,* edited by L. Fry. New York: J.F. Bergin.

Cohen, A.P., ed. 1982. *Belonging: Identity and Social Organization in British Rural Culture.* Manchester: Manchester University Press.

Denzin, N.K. 1977. "Notes on the Cuminogenic Hypothesis: A Case Study of the American Liquor Industry." *American Sociological Review* 42:905-920.

_____. 1978. "Crime and the American Liquor Industry." Pp. 87-118 in *Studies in Symbolic Interaction,* vol. 1, edited by N.K. Denzin. Greenwich, CT: JAI Press.

Deri, D. 1982. *Participation and Backlash.* Working paper submitted to the International Committee for the Evaluation of Project Renewal in Israel, Jerusalem.

_____. 1983. *Organizational Aspects of the Termination of Project Renewal.* Jerusalem: The International Committee for the Evaluation of Project Renewal.

Dozier, E.P. 1966. *Hano: A Tewa Indian Community in Arizona.* New York: Holt, Rinehart & Winston.

Eckert, J.K. 1983. "Anthropological 'Community' Studies in Aging Research." *Research on Aging* 5(4):455-472.

Erasmus, C.J. 1981. "Anarchy, Enclavement and Syntropy in Intentional and Traditional Communities." Pp. 212-227 in *Persistent People: Cultural Enclaves in Perspective,* edited by G.P. Castile and G. Kushner. Tuscon, AZ: University of Arizona Press.

Fabian, J. 1983. *Time and the Other: How Anthropology Makes its Object.* New York: Columbia University Press.

Fischer, D.H. 1978. *Growing Old in America* (Expanded ed.). New York: Oxford University Press.

Frankenberg, R. 1965. *Communities in Britain: Social Life in Town and Country.* London: Penguin.

Gans, H. 1962. *The Urban Villagers.* New York: Free Press.

_____. 1972. *People and Plans: Essays on Urban Problems and Solutions.* Harmondsworth: Penguin.

Geertz, C. 1963. "The Inegrative Revolution: Premondial Sentiments and Civil Politics in New Society." Pp. 115-157 in *Old Societies and New States,* edited by C. Geertz. New York: The Free Press.

————. 1973. "Thick Description: Toward an Interpretive Theory of Culture." Pp. 3-30 in *The Interpretation of Cultures: Selected Essays by Clifford Geertz,* edited by C. Geertz. New York: Basic Books.

————. 1979. "From the Native's Point of View: On the Nature of Anthropological Understanding." Pp. 225-241 in *Interpretive Social Science: A Reader,* edited by P. Rabinow and W.N.M. Sullivan. Berkeley, CA: University of California Press.

Gergen, K.J. 1968. "Personal Consistency and the Presentation of Self." In *The Self and Social Interaction,* edited by C. Gordon and K.J. Gergen. New York: Wiley.

Goffman, E. 1961. *Asylums.* New York: Doubleday.

Gouldner, F.H., R.R. Ritti, and T.P. Ference. 1977. "The Production of Cynical Knowledge in Organizations." *American Sociological Review* 42:539-551.

Goode, W. 1957. "Community within a Community: The Professions." *American Sociological Review* 22:194-200.

Goody, J. 1977. "Against Ritual: Loosely Structured Thoughts on a Loosely Defined Topic." Pp. 25-35 in *Secular Ritual,* edited by S.F. Moore and B.G. Myerhoff. Assen: Van Gorcum.

Gottschalk, S. 1975. *Communities and Alternatives.* Cambridge, MA: Schenkman.

Greer, S. *The Urban View.* London: Oxford University Press.

Handelman, D. 1976. "Bureaucratic Transactions: The Development of Official-Client Relationships in Israel." Pp. 223-275 in *Transaction and Meaning,* edited by B. Kapferer. Philadelphia, PA: Institute for the Study of Human Issues.

Hazan, H. 1985. "Continuity and Transformation Among the Aged: A Study in the Anthropology of Time." *Current Anthropology* 35:367-378.

Heilman, S.C. 1979. "Communication and Interaction." *Communication* 4:221-234.

Herzog, H. 1983. "The Ethnic Lists in Election 1981: An Ethnic Political Identity?" Pp. 113-138 in *The Elections in Israel— 1981,* edited by A. Arian. Tel Aviv: Ramot Publishing.

Hillery, G.A., Jr. 1968. *Communal Organization.* Chicago: University of Chicago Press.

Hochschild, A.R. 1973. *The Unexpected Community.* Englewood Cliffs, NJ: Prentice-Hall.

Hostetler, J. 1974. *Communitarian Societies.* New York: Holt, Rinehart & Winston.

Hunter, A. 1978. "Persistence of Local Sentiments in Mass Society." Pp. 133-162 in *Handbook of Contemporary Urban Life,* edited by D. Street, et al. San Francisco: Jossey-Bass.

Jacobs, J. 1974. *Fun City: An Ethnographic Study of a Retirement Community.* New York: Holt, Rinehart & Winston.

Kanter, R. 1972. *Commitment and Community: Communes and Utopia in Sociological Perspective.* Cambridge, MA: Harvard University Press.

Karp, D., G. Stone, and W. Yoels. 1977. *Being Urban.* Lexington, MA: D.C. Heath.

Keith, J. 1980. "Old Age and Community Creation." Pp. 170-197 in *Aging in Culture and Society,* edited by C.L. Fry. New York: J.F. Bergin.

————. 1982. *Old People as People: Social and Cultural Influences on Aging and Old Age.* Boston: Little, Brown.

Kling, R. and E.M. Gerson. 1978. "Patterns of Segmentation and Interaction in the Computing World." *Symbolic Interaction* 1:24-43.

Lakoff, G. and M. Johnson. 1980. *Metaphors We Live By.* Chicago: The University of Chicago Press.

Lauer, R. 1981. *Temporal Man: The Meaning and Use of Social Time.* New York: Praeger.

Leach, E. 1976. *Culture and Communication: The Logic by which Symbols are Connected.* Cambridge: Cambridge University Press.

Lewis, A. 1979. *Power, Poverty and Education.* Ramat Gan: Turtledove Publishing.

Liebow, E. 1967. *Tally's Corner.* Boston: Little, Brown.

Luckmann, B. 1970. "The Small Life Worlds of Modern Man." *Social Research* 37:580-596.

Lynd, R. and H. Lynd. 1937. *Middletown in Transaction.* New York: Harcourt Brace.

Martindale, D.A. 1964. "The Formation and Destruction of Communities." Pp. 17-87 in *Explorations in Social Change,* edited by G.K. Zollschan and W. Hirsch. Boston: Houghton-Mifflin.

Marx, E. 1976. *The Social Context of Violent Behavior: A Social Anthropological Study in an Israeli Immigrant Town.* London: Routledge & Kegan Paul.

———. 1980. "On the Anthropological Study of Nations." Pp. 15-28 in *A Composite Portrait of Israel,* edited by E. Marx. London: Academic Press.

Maxwell, R.J. 1972. "Anthropological Perspectives." Pp. 36-72 in *The Future of Time,* edited by H. Yaker, H. Osmond and F. Cheeck. New York: Anchor Books.

Moore, S.F. 1975. "Epilogue: Uncertainties in Situations: Indeterminancies in Culture." Pp. 211-239 in *Symbol and Politics in Communal Ideology,* edited by S.F. Moore and B.G. Myerhoff. Ithaca, NY: Cornell Univesity Press.

Moore, S.F. and B.G. Myerhoff, eds. 1975. *Symbol and Politics in Communal Ideology.* Ithaca, NY: Cornell University Press.

———. 1977. "Introduction: Secular Rituals—Forms and Meanings." Pp. 3-24 in *Secular Ritual,* edited by S.F. Moore and B.G. Myerhoff. Assen: Van Gorcum.

Murphy, R.D. 1971. *The Dialectics of Social Life.* New York: Basic Books.

———. 1977. *Mass Communication and Human Interaction.* Boston: Houghton Mifflin.

Musgrove, F. 1977. *Margins of the Mind.* London: Methuen.

Nisbet, R.A. 1953. *The Quest for Community.* New York: Oxford University Press.

Park, R.E. 1952. *Human Communities.* Glencoe, IL: Free Press.

Partridge, W.L. 1973. *The Hippie Ghetto.* New York: Holt, Rinehart & Winston.

Poplin, D. 1979. *Communities: A Survey of Theories and Methods of Research.* New York: Macmillan.

Redfield, R. 1955. *The Little Community.* Chicago: The University of Chicago Press.

Rogers, M.F. 1983. *Sociology, Ethnomethodology and Experience: A Phenomenological Critique.* Cambridge: Cambridge University Press.

Rosenblum, B. 1978. *Photographers at Work.* New York: Holmes and Meier.

Ross, J. 1975. "Social Borders: Definitions of Diversity." *Current Anthropology* 16:53-72.

Roth, J. 1962. *Timetables.* Indianapolis: Bobbs-Merrill.

Schimshoni, D. 1983. *Project Renewal—Policy and Execution.* Jerusalem: The International Committee for the Evaluation of Project Renewal.

Schneider, D. 1968. *American Kinship: A Cultural Account.* Englewood Cliffs, NJ: Prentice-Hall.

———. 1979. "Kinship, Community and Locality in American Culture." In *Kin and Communities,* edited by A.J. Lichtman and J.R. Challmor. Washington, DC: Smithsonian Institution.

Seeley, J. et al. 1956. *Crestwood Heights.* New York: Basic Books.

Shepher, I. 1980. "Social Boundaries of the Kibbutz." Pp. 137-178 in *A Composite Portrait of Israel,* edited by E. Marx. London: Academic Press.

Shibutani, T. 1955. "Reference Groups as Perspectives." *American Journal of Sociology* 60:562-568.

Shokeid, M. 1971. *The Dual Heritage.* Manchester: Manchester University Press.

Skorupski, J. 1976. *Symbol and Theory: A Philosophical Study of Theories of Religion in Social Anthropology.* Cambridge: Cambridge University Press.

Sperber, D. 1975. *Rethinking Symbolism.* Cambridge: Cambridge University Press.

Stacey, M. 1969. "The Myth of Community Studies." *British Journal of Sociology* 20:134-147.

Stein, M.R. 1972. *The Eclipse of Community* (Expanded ed.). Princeton, NJ: Princeton University Press.

Strathern, M. 1981. *Kinship at the Core: An Anthropology of Elmdon.* Cambridge: Cambridge Unviersity Press.

Strauss, A. 1961. *Images of the American City.* New York: Free Press.

———. 1962. "Transformations of Identity." Pp. 63-85 in *Human Behavior and Social Processes,* edited by A. Rose. Boston: Houghton Mifflin.

———. 1967. "Strategies for Discovering Urban Theory." In *Urban Research and Policy Planning,* edited by L.F. Schnore and H. Fagin. Beverly Hills, CA: Sage.

———. 1978. "A Social World Perspective." Pp. 119-128 in *Studies in Symbolic Interaction,* vol. 1, edited by N.K. Denzin. Greenwich, CT: JAI Press.

————. 1982. "Social Worlds and Legitimation Processes." Pp. 171-190 in *Studies in Symbolic Interaction,* vol. 4, edited by N.K. Denzin. Greenwich, CT: JAI Press.

Street, D. et al., eds. 1967. *Handbook of Contemporary Urban Life.* San Francisco, CA: Jossey-Bass.

Suttles, G.D. 1972. *The Social Construction of Community.* Chicago: University of Chicago Press.

Tambiah, S.J. 1979. *A Performative Approach to Ritual.* London: The British Academy.

Tilly, C. 1973. "Do Communities Act?" *Sociological Inquiry* 43:207-240.

Turner, R. 1955. "Reference Groups of Future Oriented Men." *Social Forces* 34:130-136.

Turner, V. 1969. *The Ritual Process—Structure and Anti-Structure.* Chicago: Aldine.

Unruh, D.R. 1983. *Invisible Lives: Social Worlds of the Aged.* Beverly Hills, CA: Sage.

Walsh, G. 1982. "Is Renewal Renewing?" *The Israeli Economist* (June):21-36.

Warner, W.L. and P.S. Lunt. 1941. *The Social Life of a Modern Community.* New Haven, CT: Yale University Press.

Warren, R. 1973. *The Community in America.* Chicago: Rand McNally.

Webber, M.M. 1946. "The Urban Place and the Nonplace Urban Realm." In *Explorations into Urban Structure,* edited by M.M. Webber et al. Philadelphia, PA: University of Pennsylvania Press.

Weingrod, A. 1966. *Reluctant Pioneers: Village Development in Israel.* Ithaca, NY: Cornell University Press.

————. 1979. "Recent Trends in Israeli Ethnicity." *Ethnic and Social Studies* 2:55-65.

Whyte, W.F. 1955. *Street Corner Society.* Chicago: University of Chicago Press.

Wiener, C. 1981. *The Politics of Alcoholism.* New Brunswick, NJ: Transaction.

Williams, R. 1983. "Community." Pp. 75-76 in *Keywords,* edited by R. Williams. London: Fontana.

Wirth, L. 1928. *The Ghetto.* Chicago: University of Chicago Press.

Yancey, W.L., E.P. Ericksen, and R.N. Juliani. 1976. "Emergent Ethnicity: A Review and Reformulation." *American Sociological Review* 41:391-413.

Zerubavel, E. 1981. *Hidden Rhythms*. Chicago: University of Chicago Press.

Subject Index